PETWORTH

West Sussex

National Trust

Acknowledgements

For help with this guidebook, I wish to pay special tribute to the late Gervase Jackson-Stops, whose research and publications form its foundations. Everyone who writes about Petworth must acknowledge the kindness of Lord Egremont, who has allowed the fullest access to his family papers and who has commented upon the text. The private archive is administered by Mrs Alison McCann of the West Sussex Record Office, whose advice has been invaluable. The Duke of Northumberland has also generously permitted study of the manuscripts and accounts held at Alnwick Castle. For help with research, I am particularly grateful to Tracey Avery, Geoffrey Fremont-Barnes, Carolyn Knight, Charles O'Brien, Nino Strachey, the late Jean Thomas and Margaret Wynter. The picture entries are based on notes compiled by St John Gore and Alastair Laing (who has helped in a variety of other ways). I am also indebted for scholarly information to Sir Geoffrey de Bellaigue, Anthony du Boulay, Peter Brears, David Connell, John Cushion, Martin Drury, Alfred Fisher, Ruth Guilding, John Hart, Kay Holmes, David Howarth, Simon Jervis, Harriet Jordan, Tim Knox, John Mills, Jeremy Pearson, Sylvia Sumira, Gerard Vaughan, Susan Walker, Anthony Wells-Cole and Dyfri Williams. At Petworth, I have received much assistance from Diana Owen and Nicky Ingram. Oliver Garnett edited the guide and drew up the family tree.

Christopher Rowell

Photographs: Country Life Picture Library p. 71; Christopher Dalton p. 51; Macmillan Publishers p. 94; National Trust pp. 47, 56, 75, 81, 95; National Trust Christina Beckett, National Trust Images pp. 36, 52, Bill Batten p. 45, A. C. Cooper pp. 18, 38, 61, 68, 79, 84; by courtesy of Lord Egremont pp. 28, 36, 58, 91, Stuart Cox back cover, Andreas von Einsiedel pp. 5, 13, 15, 23, 24, 27, 43, 66, Roy Fox p. 32, John Hammond pp. 1, 11, 28, 40, 44, 62, 69, 78, 83, 91, Matthew Hollow front cover, Rupert Truman pp. 7, 55, 70 (bottom), Jeremy Whitaker pp. 25, 33, Derrick E. Witty pp. 20, 39, 57, 63, 64, 65, 67, 72, 73, 88, His Grace the Duke of Northumberland p. 59; Royal Institute of British Architects/British Architectural Library p. 70 (top); Trustees of the Tate Gallery pp. 10, 31, 35, 49, 77, 85, 87; by courtesy of the West Sussex Record Office p. 93; Tate, London p.30.

First published in Great Britain in 1997 by the National Trust
© 1997 The National Trust
Registered charity no. 205846

ISBN 978-1-84359-026-2
Revised 1999, 2000, 2002, 2006, 2017;
Reprinted 2004, 2007, 2008, 2009, 2011, 2012, 2019
Designed by James Shurmer
Phototypeset in Monotype Bembo Series 270
by Printessential Limited, Smallfield, Surrey (SG1087)
Printed by Acorn Press, Swindon for National Trust (Enterprises) Ltd,
Heelis, Kemble Drive, Swindon, Wilts SN2 2NA
on Revive Silk made from 100% recycled paper

(*Front cover*) The Brussels Picture Gallery, by Dans Teniers the Younger, 1651

(*Title-page*) A carved and gilded winged angel in the Chapel created by the Proud Duke

(*Back cover*) Sculpture of Apollo by John Flaxman RA, 1825. It was Lord Egremont's first commission of an ideal subject, and depicts Apollo as the protector of shepherds

CONTENTS

PETWORTH HOUSE

Constable called Petworth 'the house of art', and it still contains the National Trust's finest collection of pictures and sculpture.

Petworth has passed by inheritance since 1150, when it came into the Percy family. The history of the Percy dynasty is a chronicle of power leading not only to high honours (the earldom of Northumberland in 1377), but also to death and dishonour. The Percy castle was repaired and extended by the 8th, 9th and 10th Earls of Northumberland in the late sixteenth and early seventeenth centuries. The 9th Earl was a notable scholar and bibliophile, whose son, the 10th Earl, a friend and patron of Van Dyck, founded the Petworth picture collection in the 1630s.

The 10th Earl's granddaughter, Elizabeth, as the Percy heiress, was married in 1682 to Charles Seymour, 6th Duke of Somerset, who rebuilt Petworth with her money. Nicknamed the 'Proud Duke', he looked to Versailles as the inspiration of the present palace, which was probably designed by Daniel Marot and was largely completed by 1702. A patron (most notably of Grinling Gibbons) and a collector, the Duke employed royal craftsmen in the rebuilding and refurnishing of Petworth. His formal gardens, laid out by the royal gardener George London, were replaced in the 1750s by one of 'Capability' Brown's most poetic 'natural' landscapes, immortalised in Turner's paintings. Brown's employer, Charles Wyndham, 2nd Earl of Egremont, inherited Petworth through his mother (a daughter of the Proud Duke). His collection of Old Master pictures was displayed at Egremont House, Piccadilly, and most of his antique statuary at Petworth. The 2nd Earl was also a prominent Whig politician, serving as the equivalent of Foreign Secretary from 1762 till his untimely death in 1763.

Then began what has been called Petworth's golden age – the 74-year reign of the 2nd Earl's son, George O'Brien Wyndham, 3rd Earl of Egremont. A great agriculturalist, philanthropist and one of the most successful racehorse owners in the history of the turf, the benevolent and enigmatic 3rd Earl is famous as the host to a whole generation of British artists. A multitude of paintings and sculptures by Turner and his contemporaries remains as a testament to the 3rd Earl's generosity as a patron. He extended his father's North Gallery twice between 1824 and 1827 as the collection grew. Almost every room was altered and continuously rearranged in a restless search for perfection that culminated in his enlargement and elaboration of Grinling Gibbons's Carved Room.

After the 3rd Earl's death in 1837, his natural son, George, made few changes and was created Lord Leconfield in 1859. His son, Henry, 2nd Lord Leconfield, commissioned Anthony Salvin to make considerable alterations, principally at the south end of the house and in the Carved Room. In 1947 Charles, 3rd Lord Leconfield gave the house and park with an endowment to the National Trust, thus ensuring their permanent preservation. The 3rd Lord Leconfield's nephew and heir, John Wyndham, offered a large proportion of the contents to the Treasury in lieu of the tax payable on his uncle's death in 1952. Wyndham was created Lord Egremont in 1963 for his services as Harold Macmillan's private secretary, and in 1967 succeeded his father as 6th Lord Leconfield. His son, Max, 2nd Lord Egremont and 7th Lord Leconfield, lives at Petworth with his family.

With the collaboration of Lord and Lady Egremont, who have generously loaned numerous pictures, and with the benefit of an anonymous donation, the National Trust has embarked upon the redecoration and rearrangement of the state rooms following extensive research into their history.

The 2nd Earl's statuary in the North Gallery

CHAPTER ONE
TOUR OF THE HOUSE

The Exterior

THE EAST FRONT AND COURTYARD

The 6th Duke of Somerset refronted only the south (left-hand) end of the rear, east front during his remodelling of Petworth at the end of the seventeenth century. As a result, the mish-mash of different styles visible here clearly reveals the long and complicated genesis of Petworth.

To the north (to the right as one faces the east front) is the pointed arch of the Chapel's east window, the tracery of which is probably nineteenth-century. The Chapel, probably built *c.*1309, was largely remodelled by the Proud Duke (1685–92). Above the Chapel window is another large opening lighting the Old Library, constructed by the 6th Duke in *c.*1702–3 and used by Turner as a studio. To the south (or left) of the Chapel is a doorway leading into the Luggage Corridor, presumably the access point for guests' belongings. To the left again is the doorway by which National Trust visitors enter the house via the Oak Staircase Hall. To the left are the sash-windows, lengthened in 1815, which light the Somerset Room and Square Dining Room. Then, separated by one of several buttresses, come the two tall round-headed sash-windows of the Grand Staircase, installed after 1718 when the Staircase was rebuilt after the fire of 1714. Previously there was a single 'greate window'. From there to the south corner, the façade is of Portland stone, originally constructed by the 6th Duke, and repaired both at the beginning of the nineteenth century and during Salvin's extensive remodelling of this end of the house between 1869 and 1872.

Salvin replaced the 3rd Earl's conservatory (1821) with the stone screen and gateway that bisect the courtyard and separate the public and private sides of the house. At the opposite (north) end of the courtyard he also demolished another conservatory, an adjacent real tennis court and a passage connecting the North Gallery with the Servants' Block. The courtyard was, therefore, previously cut off from the Pleasure Ground. It was known as the Fountain Court after the Coade stone circular fountain in the form of a triton blowing a conch shell (after a model by the sixteenth-century Italian sculptor Giambologna) which was removed to the garden below the south front in 1872, probably as part of Salvin's alterations.

THE NORTH FRONT

Jutting out from the north end of the main block are the 3rd Earl's extensions (1824–7) to his father's North Gallery (1754–63). The recently reconstructed skylights can be clearly seen, as can the round-headed thermal windows which preceded them, before being blocked up inside to provide more picture-hanging space. The original gallery was formed by fenestrating the tall round-headed arches of the late seventeenth-century cloister which ran the full width of the north front, and above it the 6th Duke of Somerset refaced the façade of the main building with distinctive rustication reminiscent of engravings in Rubens's *Palazzi di Genova*. The Duke had the 1652 edition of this famous book in his library – the 'Facciata [façade] del Palazzo K...' has pilasters with diamond rustication of the same proportions. The arcade or cloister beneath was presumably also refaced in the same style by the 6th Duke, and was probably similar to the rusticated arches and pillars of the north front of Boughton, Northamptonshire, rebuilt in the 1690s and early 1700s for Ralph Montagu, later 1st Duke of Montagu, probably to the design of Daniel Marot. In 1749/50 the 'North Cloisters' were furnished with '4 Marble Tables on Walnuttree frames' and '6 broken cane chairs'. In the Proud Duke's day, the cloister faced an enclosed orange garden the width of the house, with an orangery at the far end. The lawn here is still called the Orange Green.

The west front

THE WEST FRONT

Entirely rebuilt by the 6th Duke of Somerset between *c*.1688 and 1702, the west front, 320 feet long, can only be described as palatial. It was conceived as the visitor's first impression of the house, being approached through iron gates via an enclosed courtyard with a circular carriage drive leading to the front door in the centre. Its architect is unknown, but the Huguenot architect and designer Daniel Marot probably played the major role in its conception. Although the west front of Petworth has been considerably altered since the Duke's day, it remains one of the most impressive English translations of the European Baroque style.

A painting of *c*.1710 in the collection of the Duke of Rutland (illustrated on p. 71) reveals its original appearance. The central three bays were surmounted by a flat-roofed square dome encompassed by a stone and 'ironwork bellcony' (as it was described in 1697) supporting urns. The shape of the dome recalls Marot's designs for the Paleis Wassenaar-Obdam at The Hague, and Montagu House, Bloomsbury, rebuilt for Ralph Montagu after 1686. The parapet of the façade consisted, as it still does, of a wall punctuated by stone balustrades above the windows. Originally, however, full-length statues stood above the three-windowed central bay and the corner pavilions, with carved stone urns in between. Above the ground-floor windows, the corner pavilions retain pairs of busts flanking the ducal phoenix crest.

Work began in about 1688, but the first references to the west front occur in 1689–90, when Samuel Foulkes, the mason, was paid 'towards the frontice-peece in the new Buildings' and John Selden was also paid for the 'keystones with carved winges' (the Duke's crest) above each window. In 1690 a bill was presented 'for slatting ye Sirculer roofe' – presumably the dome. In 1692 Grinling Gibbons was paid 'for statues': perhaps those originally surmounting the west front. If so, these must have been made of lead, judging by the painters' bill of 1697 'for 12 figures painted on the ffront of the House' (ie four statues on each of the two end pavilions and over the central frontispiece).

The fire of 1714 apparently destroyed the central dome, but as a dome is still shown in a sketch of *c*.1770, it must have been rebuilt soon afterwards – other repairs seem to have been completed by about 1720. The dome was removed by the 3rd Earl of Egremont, possibly in 1777–8 when a mason, John Gilliam, working under the direction of Matthew Brettingham the Younger, was paid for 'working and setting of sand stone on the Parrapet and setting D° in the west front'. Certainly, the 3rd Earl gave the façade its present guise, although his pediment over the central three bays has since been removed. As well as simplifying the roof line, he extended the ground-floor windows so that one could step out of them on to a new stone terrace. Previously, guests had had to jump from the original higher window sills across an area lighting the basement, which had caused 'some awkward accidents'.

The Interior

THE WHITE OR OAK STAIRCASE

Since at least 1743 this has been the tourists' entrance to the house and still serves as such today because the two principal entrances – the seventeenth-century Marble Hall and the nineteenth-century Stone Hall – cannot now be used for visitors. Part of the original manor house, the staircase was remodelled by the 6th Duke of Somerset around 1700. The wood is oak and may originally have been unpainted, but after alterations were made in softwood, the panelled dado and the balustrade were painted a grey white. A simple form of oak graining was probably introduced in the early eighteenth century, which seems to have survived until the mid-nineteenth century, when the panelling and the balustrade were regrained to match the unpainted oak of the banister rail. It was first called the 'Oak Staircase' in 1869. By 1925 only the balustrade and the panelling supporting the staircase were grained, and blue and white wallpaper of a loosely Neoclassical design had been hung; this scheme was repeated in 1997. The previous wall colours are unknown, but as the room was called the White Staircase by 1795, it was presumably a white or stony white, colours typical of Petworth around 1800.

In 1795 stairs were constructed down to the cellars (presumably cutting through the below-stairs armoury closet) to link up with the subterranean passage leading to the kitchens and Servants' Block. A door was installed at the head of the new stairs into the adjacent Somerset Room, which acted as a servery for the Square Dining Room beyond. This made the room a more efficient link between kitchens and dining-room. The great doorway (now blocked) opposite the courtyard entrance originally led into the Carved Room, which in 1743 was the first room shown to visitors and which also served as a dining-room from about 1795.

PAST FURNISHINGS

In the 6th Duke's time (as recorded in 1749/50), this was the 'Lobby Staircase', hung with 66 pictures in gilt, or black and gilt, frames. In 1764 it was called the 'Picture Stair Case' and 34 pictures were hung here. A closet under the stairs contained 'about one hundred Musketts, Sixty Halberds, Sixty Pistoles, and Twelve Swords all very Old', some of which must have come from the Proud Duke's Servants' Hall. Otherwise, apart from a sedan chair, a 'Wainscott Reading Desk' and two mahogany card-tables, the room was unfurnished. It was lit by a hanging lantern and 'two tin Lanthorns on the Stairs with Circular Glass Fronts'. By 1869 a mahogany dining-table in four parts, with two stands 'for extra leaves', stood here in case it was needed elsewhere.

FURNITURE

The Victorian mahogany weighing-scales were listed here in 1869.

The longcase clock is by Thomas Tompion (1639–1713), the most famous of seventeenth-century English clockmakers. It cost £16 12s, which was paid to Tompion's executor, George Graham, in 1713. In 1749/50 it stood in the lobby next to the Grand Staircase.

PORCELAIN

IN CABINET:

Pieces from a service, English, Coalport factory, *c.*1805.

THE SOMERSET ROOM

Presumably named after the 6th Duke of Somerset, this room originally formed part of the Duke's much larger Servants' Hall, which the 2nd Earl of Egremont converted into a dining-room. When the present Square Dining Room next door was created by the 3rd Earl about 1795, the Somerset Room was intended for the display of pictures and sculpture, and as a servery. Food would have been warmed up here before transfer into the Square Dining Room. By 1869 it had become the Oak Dining Room.

PAST FURNISHINGS

The 3rd Earl's accounts indicate that the Somerset Room was probably the first location of his shrine to Napoleon – a new doorway from 'Bonaparte's Room' to the Square Dining Room was made in 1812 and it still had this name in 1837. Turner's view of *c.*1827 (illustrated on p. 10) shows the room thickly hung with pictures and with antique statuary in the corners of the room.

DECORATION

The room was redecorated in 1995–6 in accordance with analysis of the 3rd Earl's original paint schemes. Turner's view shows that the Somerset Room and adjacent Square Dining Room were painted *en suite* in white with dark skirting boards. This has been repeated, although the original warm white is now deeper and stonier to take account of the faded contents of the room.

CHIMNEYPIECE

The marble chimneypiece is probably one of the 'five marble chimneypieces at Petworth House £40 each' made by the sculptor J. E. Carew (1785–1868).

PRINCIPAL PICTURES

FIREPLACE WALL:

LEFT, BELOW:

114 AELBERT CUYP (1620–91)
Imaginary Landscape with Cattle, Huntsmen and a Horseman
Probably painted in the mid-1650s, and perhaps inspired by the landscape near Nijmegen, in east Holland, it was bought by the 3rd Earl between 1829 and 1834.

OVER CHIMNEYPIECE, TOP:

149 Sir PETER LELY (1618–80)
The Younger Children of Charles I
The children are (left to right): Henry, Duke of Gloucester, aged eight; Elizabeth, aged twelve; and James, Duke of York (the future James II), aged fourteen. The picture was commissioned in 1647 by the 10th Earl of Northumberland, in whose custody the children were placed after the fall of Oxford, and was painted at Syon. It was lent to the King during his imprisonment at Hampton Court.

BELOW:

272–9 ADAM ELSHEIMER (1578–1610)
Saints and Prophets from the Old and New Testaments
On copper
Elsheimer's exquisite landscape settings inspired Claude: compare them with Claude's great landscape (no. 329) opposite. They were acquired in 1645 by the 10th Earl of Northumberland from the famous collection of the 1st Duke of Buckingham. Originally, the full set of pictures (at least ten, rather than eight) probably adorned a cabinet. They are the 'Eight little pictures in one frame by Elshamer'

valued at £250 at Northumberland House in 1671. In 1752 they were placed in individual Rococo frames by Joseph Duffour, which have recently been returned to them within a modern glazed frame as protection.

RIGHT OF FIREPLACE, BELOW:

LOWER REGISTER

298 TITAN (*c*.1487/90–1576)
Man in a Black Plumed Hat
Probably painted *c*.1515–20 and possibly listed at Petworth in 1671, this is an undoubted original despite its abraded surface.

END WALL, OPPOSITE WINDOWS:

667 BERNARDO BELLOTTO (1722–80)
The Capitol, Rome
Bellotto's paintings are much rarer in England than those of his master and uncle, Canaletto. This picture, painted *c*.1742, is probably the 'View in Rome' by 'Canaletti' inherited in 1774 by the 3rd Earl from his uncle, the Earl of Thomond.

MAIN WALL, OPPOSITE FIREPLACE:

EXTREME LEFT, BELOW:

63 Attributed to HIERONYMUS BOSCH (*c*.1450–1516)
The Adoration of the Kings
This is a high-quality, possibly, autograph variant of the central panel of Bosch's triptych of the *Epiphany* of *c*.1495 in the Prado, Madrid.

OPPOSITE:

329 CLAUDE GELLÉE, known as CLAUDE
(1600–82)
Landscape with Jacob and Laban
Genesis (XXIX, v.16–20) tells the story of Jacob's love for the beautiful Rachel, whom he eventually married as a reward for his long service to her father, Laban, depicted here flanked by Rachel and his elder daughter, Leah. Painted in Rome in 1654 for Carlo Cardelli (1626–62) and bought in London c.1686 by the 6th Duke.

TOP REGISTER, LEFT OF CENTRE:

154 Attributed to TITIAN (c.1487/90–1576) and another hand
'Naked Venus and a Satyr'
Acquired, perhaps via Van Dyck, by the 10th Earl of Northumberland. In 1652 it was described as a 'Mars and Venus', but it was damaged and partially repainted between then and 1671, when it was listed with its present title. Its poor condition makes the 1652 attribution to Titian difficult to confirm.

RIGHT OF CENTRE:

83 PAUL BRIL (1554–1626)
Landscape with Troglodyte Goatherds
Bril, a Fleming who worked in Rome from the 1570s, was influenced by Italian landscape paintings and by Annibale Carracci in particular. Probably painted c.1610–15, when he had begun working on a larger scale on canvas, after previously specialising in small pictures on panel or copper. It was bought in 1754 by the 2nd Earl for £126. The frame is early eighteenth-century French.

48 JACOB VAN RUISDAEL (1629/30–82)
A Waterfall

The Somerset Room; watercolour-gouache by J. M. W. Turner, c.1827 (Tate)

St John the Baptist; by Adam Elsheimer (nos. 272–9; Somerset Room)

SCULPTURE

ON PIER-TABLE:

85 *Venus de Medici*: an eighteenth-century Italian or French bronze reduction of the famous Antique statue (thought to be a first-century BC copy after a lost early third-century bronze of the school of Praxiteles) in the Uffizi, Florence.

FURNITURE

The giltwood sofa and chairs (from a much larger set) are attributed to Thomas Chippendale, who certainly supplied the 3rd Earl with furniture in 1779. In 1764 the set was split between the White and Gold Room and the King of Spain's Bedchamber, and was originally decorated in white and gold (the regilding is nineteenth-century) and covered with 'Crimson Silk Damask and Brass naild'.

LEFT OF FIREPLACE:

The writing-table decorated with Boulle-work is French, *c.*1690, in the manner of André-Charles Boulle (1642–1732), Louis XIV's *ébéniste*, who gave his name to this form of inlaid decoration.

RIGHT OF FIREPLACE:

The writing-table decorated with Boulle-work of pewter and tortoiseshell inlays on a brass ground is in the manner of Gerrit Jensen (active 1680–d.1715), but stamped by a later cabinetmaker, Charles-Michel Cochois (d.1765).

BETWEEN WINDOWS:

The giltwood pier-glass was supplied to the 2nd Earl of Egremont by James Whittle (active 1731–d.1759) and is similar to a pair of pier-glasses at Holkham, Norfolk, attributed to Whittle by Matthew Brettingham in 1761.

The giltwood pier-table is French in the Louis XVI style, *c.*1785, and is stamped by the Parisian cabinetmaker Jean-Baptiste-Claude Sené (1747–1803; *maître* 1769), one of the principal suppliers to the French court.

END WALL:

OPPOSITE WINDOWS:

The giltwood side-table is English, *c.*1755.

IN SOUTH-WEST CORNER:

The four-fold screen is made up of panels of early eighteenth-century Dutch or Spanish leather.

PORCELAIN

ON TABLE OPPOSITE WINDOWS:

Two 'assiettes à soupe' (soup plates) from a set of eighteen in *décor 'fleurs filets bleu'* (flowers and blue ribbons) supplied to the 3rd Earl of Egremont by the Sèvres factory on 13 September 1774. Both are marked 'LB' for the painter Jean-Nicolas Le Bel *jeune* (1749–after 1816).

The matching wine-cooler is one of two '*Seaux à bouteille*' in this *décor* which the 3rd Earl also acquired from Sèvres in 1774. Also marked 'BD'.

ON CHIMNEYPIECE:

Two 'Seaux crenelés' ('crenellated buckets', ie monteiths – for cooling wine glasses): these are probably the '*2 Seaux crenellés*' in *décor 'fleurs filets*

bleu' (flowers and blue ribbons), made in 1773 and supplied direct from Sèvres to the 3rd Earl of Egremont on 13 September 1774. Both marked 'BD' for the gilder François Baudouin *père* (fl.1750–1800).

ON LEDGE IN CORNER:

A large Chinese bulbous bottle decorated with an overall raised white slip design on a celadon ground; *c.*1800. This may be the 'fine Sea Green China jar' for which the 3rd Earl paid 12 guineas in 1810 to 'Fogg, China Man, No.16, Warwick St, Golden Square, London'.

FLANKING FIREPLACE:

A pair of Chinese famille rose baluster two-handled vases, *c.*1830.

CHANDELIER

The ormolu colza oil chandelier was made *c.*1825 for the North Gallery, and is one of a pair that hung at either end of the South Corridor.

THE SQUARE DINING ROOM

This was originally part of the Proud Duke's rather bigger Servants' Hall, adjacent Butler's Pantry and Servants' Staircases, which were converted by the 2nd Earl into a dining-room and a vestibule to the Grand Staircase, containing statuary in 1764. The present Square Dining Room was constructed by the 3rd Earl probably in about 1795. The panelling was installed in 1799, and the windows were raised in height by one pane in 1815. Curiously, the 3rd Earl seems always to have had a thick hang of pictures here, as they hang awkwardly across the fielded woodwork.

Turner's watercolour-gouache of *c.*1827 (see p. 85) shows Reynolds's great *Macbeth and the Witches* (no. 61; 1786) as the centrepiece of columns of smaller pictures and surmounted by an oval portrait precariously canted out over the cornice. This pattern has been copied, making the Square Dining Room an immensely rare re-creation of a picture-hang recorded by Turner. The arrangement of furniture and sculpture in Turner's view has also been repeated. Interestingly, the inventory taken in 1764 (following the 2nd Earl's death) describes in several rooms similar arrangements of side-tables, flanked by blue-and-white china jars (acquired

by the Duchess of Somerset around 1700) and supporting Antique marble busts. In this respect the 3rd Earl clearly perpetuated his father's style of display, while continually moving the pictures. The 1837 inventory lists the furniture depicted in Turner's watercolour-gouache and confirms that, when not in use, the dining table was dismantled and stored next door in the Somerset Room.

By 1869, the room had become a drawing-room, but the mid-eighteenth-century and later marble-topped side-tables (three of which were already here in 1764) remained in place, together with the blue-and-white china (and presumably the sculpture) shown in Turner's watercolour. The picture-hang (even more crowded than in Turner's view) remained as recorded in about 1840 until 1952, when Anthony Blunt grouped the Van Dycks together here in a much less crowded arrangement.

DECORATION

The original warm white with dark skirting boards, shown in Turner's *c.*1827 view, was repeated in 1993–4, following paint analysis. As in the adjoining Somerset Room, the 3rd Earl's colour scheme was interpreted in a browner tone, more in keeping with the contents of the room. This is the third colour scheme since the 3rd Earl's day. A green and buff scheme was introduced by the 2nd

Lord Leconfield in the course of Salvin's alterations of *c.*1869–72. It was replaced in the 1950s by John Fowler, who stippled the panelling in yellow and picked out the mouldings in white.

CHIMNEYPIECE

*The chimneypiece c.*1755–60 of yellow Siena and white Carrara marble, is similar to a chimneypiece formerly at Northumberland House, London, which has been attributed to Joseph Pickford (active 1714–60), who supplied chimneypieces to Egremont House, Piccadilly. It was installed by the 2nd Lord Leconfield in 1878–9.

PELMETS

The three carved wood pelmets and pendants were placed here by the 2nd Lord Leconfield *c.*1869–72. The central pelmet was made at that time to copy the two flanking pelmets, which were moved from the Carved Room. The Carved Room pelmets were made for the 3rd Earl of Egremont, probably between *c.*1830 and 1837, by Jonathan Ritson, a local carver who worked at Petworth *c.*1827–43. The central pelmet is the work of the estate carpenter Henry Hoad, who embellished it by carving a mallard shot by Lord Leconfield.

CURTAINS

The deep crimson festoon curtains of stamped mohair velvet were presumably hung by the 2nd Lord Leconfield *c.*1869–72, and replaced his father's '3 pʳˢ rich figured satin lined curtains with shaped valances and gilt cornices', which in turn had replaced the 3rd Earl's crimson silk damask festoons depicted by Turner in *c.*1827 and described in the 1837 inventory.

PRINCIPAL PICTURES

FIREPLACE WALL:

RIGHT OF FIREPLACE, MIDDLE:

223 Sir ANTHONY VAN DYCK (1599–1641)
Henry Percy, 9th Earl of Northumberland, the 'Wizard Earl' (1564–1632)
A scholar and scientist who spent many years in the Tower after being implicated in the Gunpowder Plot, he is depicted in academical robes (he was created MA of Oxford, 1605) in a pose suggesting wisdom. His alchemical experiments gained him his nickname. Painted posthumously for his son, the 10th Earl.

WALL OPPOSITE FIREPLACE, CENTRE:

61 Sir JOSHUA REYNOLDS, PRA (1723–92)
Macbeth and the Witches
This huge, unfinished and much deteriorated painting was commissioned in 1786 by Alderman Boydell for his Shakespeare Gallery in London. The 3rd Earl must have acquired it after the gallery's contents were dispersed by lottery in 1804.

WEST WALL, OPPOSITE WINDOWS:

RIGHT SIDE, BOTTOM REGISTER:

300 Sir ANTHONY VAN DYCK (1599–1641)
Mountjoy Blount, 1st Earl of Newport (1597–1665/6), George, Lord Goring (1608–57) and a Page, Royalist officers and close friends. Perhaps painted to commemorate their preparations for the Scottish campaign of 1639.

FURNITURE

AROUND ROOM:

The five carved and white painted side-tables with marble tops are probably of different dates, although they appear to be a set. The pair on either side of the fireplace are probably the originals of *c.*1735 (ie perhaps the '2 Marble Side board Tables' in the Proud Duke's Dining Room; the present Beauty Room). The 1764 inventory describes the 'Large Side-Board Table' opposite as 'Carv'd & Painted white to Match the other two', which implies that it was made for the 2nd Earl between 1750 and 1763. The pair flanking the door to the Marble Hall was not listed in 1764 and may have been added by the 3rd Earl.

BETWEEN WINDOWS:

The carved giltwood pier-glasses and marble-topped tables are certainly attributable to James Whittle, who, with his partner and successor Samuel Norman (active 1746–67), supplied so much furniture to the 2nd Earl. These pier-glasses were probably listed in the Dining Room in the 1764 inventory (but at that date the pier-tables were larger and parcel-gilt). The present tables are presumably the 'Marble top console tables' listed in 1869.

ON PIER-TABLES:

The pair of ormolu and opaque glass colza oil lamps is *c.*1820.

ON CHIMNEYPIECE:

The Boulle bracket clock with ormolu mounts is French, Louis XIV, *c.*1700. It is surmounted by an ormolu figure of Fame and the dial incorporates a profile portrait of the King. Signed by the Parisian clockmaker Nicolas Delaunay (d.1743).

OVER CHIMNEYPIECE:

The carved giltwood glass was installed here probably by the 2nd Lord Leconfield in 1869–72 (it was not listed here in 1869). It is probably by Whittle and Norman, being listed in 1764 as a pier-glass in the King of Spain's Bedchamber, which was refurbished by the 2nd Earl in the 1750s. The 1764 inventory reads: 'A Large Carv'd & gilt Glass fraime with Glass Borders & 4 Plates in Dᵒ'.

PORCELAIN

FLANKING SIDE-TABLE OPPOSITE FIREPLACE:

The large blue-and-white porcelain jars are Chinese, Kangxi period (1662–1722), and were purchased by the 6th Duke and Duchess around 1700. Such vases were coveted status symbols: in 1717 Augustus the Strong, King of Saxony, exchanged a regiment of dragoons for 151 pieces of porcelain, including 18 vases similar to those at Petworth. An arrangement of blue-and-white jars and the 'oval marble sarcophagus' (wine cooler) beneath the table was recorded here in 1837.

The picture hang on the south wall of the Square Dining Room has recently been restored following Turner's view of c.1827 (illustrated on p. 85). It is centred on Reynolds's Macbeth and the Witches *(no. 61)*

The Marble Hall

THE MARBLE HALL

The Marble Hall was built as the main entrance to the house for the 6th Duke. It was probably designed by Daniel Marot, having close similarities with the Trèveszaal, or audience chamber, of the States General, which he added to the Binnenhof Palace in The Hague in 1696–8. Work was largely completed in 1692, when John Burton was paid for 'the great doors that is in front of the house giveing into the hall of State'. In the same year James Sayers, mason, indented for 'paving the Hall of State with black and white marble', which was brought from Purbeck. The pattern was taken (and elaborated) from C. A. d'Aviler's *Cours complet d'architecture* (1691), one of the most popular of seventeenth-century pattern-books. The carver John Selden was responsible for the robustly three-dimensional decorative woodwork, including the Somerset coats of arms above the chimneypieces, flanked by the ducal supporters: a bull and a unicorn. The panelling was put up by Thomas Larkin. The brass lock-plates here and elsewhere are also chased with the Duke's arms and were made by the locksmith John Draper. The plasterer Edward Goudge was paid 'in pte for the hall of State', so it is curious that the ceiling is plain, unlike his coffered ceiling for the Chapel. Perhaps it was a casualty of the 1714 fire. John Madgwick made the great niches that flank the Square Dining Room door with its cleverly foreshortened perspective, a particularly Baroque conceit. The niches must have been intended for statuary, and the colossal Roman figures of the first and second century AD are probably the '2 Marble Statues on Marble Pedestals' listed here in 1749/50 and were definitely *in situ* by 1764.

The Marble Hall has been little changed since the 6th Duke's time and is full of French and Dutch reminiscences: the marble skirtings are a particularly Dutch feature. The full-blown Baroque style is rare in England, and the room as a whole, like Wren's work at Hampton Court, derives (via Holland) from the grandeur of the palatial interiors commissioned by Louis XIV. This impression would have been all the greater if Selden's '2 large pannells which were designed for the Hall of State' had not been 'set by'. Perhaps one found a new home in the 3rd Earl's Carved Room, where the carved panel on the central pier, celebrating the 6th Duke's royal descent, would have married well with the armorials over the Marble Hall chimneypieces.

The 1st Lord Leconfield made the room into a comfortable study after his wife's death in 1863, having been asked by the housekeeper, Mrs Smith, to move temporarily to the south end during spring-cleaning. He never moved back, and the rooms between the Marble Hall and the south front became his private sanctum where he also slept. Madeline Wyndham's watercolour of *c.*1865 (illustrated on p. 91) shows how he had made himself comfortable in this vast room. According to Constance Leconfield: 'in 1867 this had long been disused [as the main entrance], owing to the draughts caused by the doors being opened.' The double-glazing of the porch is presumably mid-nineteenth-century. In the early 1870s Salvin built a new entrance hall on the east side for Constance's husband, the 2nd Lord Leconfield, to provide a more sheltered and private access facing the town. Lord and Lady Leconfield were responsible for the present pale green applied *c.*1869–72; the original colour was a stony white.

PAST FURNISHINGS

In 1749/50 the furniture was black and gold: two of the group of five marble-topped tables and the eighteen *sgabello* hall chairs (all still at Petworth). The room was lit by '8 guilt Sconces for Candles'. There were '4 Pictures in Pannels over ye Doors and Chimneys' (ie set into the panelling). The 2nd Earl removed the black and gold furniture, replacing it with 'Eight Hall Stools'. The number of pictures had increased to six portraits (again over the doors and chimneys, but now also over the 'False Doors'), including four likenesses of philosophers: Calvin and Luther (both moved to the North Gallery by the 3rd Earl and now restored there) and Molinass [*sic*] and Spinosa. In 1802 window curtains were put up (presumably the red-fringed draperies shown in Phillips's portrayal of the Allied Sovereigns' visit in 1814) and there was a 'square Persian Carpet' in 1837 which may have been laid as early as 1804. By the time of Turner's sketches of the room (*c.*1827), it doubled as a billiard-room (the billiard-table was mended in 1836 and was still here in 1869).

During the 3rd Earl's lifetime, the Marble Hall was filled with pictures which were hung in tiers in all the available panels, not just over the chimneys and doors. A similar arrangement, dating from *c.*1840, survived until 1952, when Anthony Blunt reverted (unwittingly) to 1764 levels (over

doors and chimneypieces only). The 3rd Earl also increased the number of statues, and the present display alludes to this. There was a flurry of statue-moving in 1832, when plinths, pedestals and statuary were redeployed and there was also 'an alteration to niches in the Marble Hall'. By 1837 there were only two marble busts (of Pitt and Fox by Nollekens) and a small bronze, plus the large statues in the niches.

In 1869, when the room was Lord Leconfield's study, it was furnished with tables, reading stands, writing materials and comfortable upholstered seat furniture, in addition to the billiard-table.

FURNITURE

The pair of black and gold tables with marble tops is probably Florentine, *c*.1690, and was listed here in 1749/50: '2 Marble Tables on black & gilt frames'. They are from a group of five similar tables, of which three have five legs, the central leg providing extra support to the heavy marble top, but also perhaps to allow for the display of marble busts.

The black and gold decoration has been renewed, probably in the nineteenth century.

The four painted stools are English, *c*.1760, and may be from a set of eight described here in 1764; 'Eight Hall Stools with Coat of Arms painted on the Seat.' If so, they have been repainted, probably when the present décor was applied by the 2nd Lord Leconfield.

The inlaid mahogany organ was made in 1786 by John England (active 1764–90) and the 3rd Earl paid £169 15s on 25 December 1786. Its mechanism was removed in about 1914, but still survives (in part).

PRINCIPAL SCULPTURE

IN ROUND-HEADED NICHES:

These are probably the '2 Marble Statues' listed here in 1749/50 (and they were certainly here in 1791), which suggests that they were acquired by the Proud Duke, who incorporated the niches in his original construction of the Marble Hall and who is known to have bought several pieces of antique sculpture.

TO LEFT AND RIGHT:

No. 56, of Italian marble, dating from the second century AD, possibly depicts the Procurator of an eastern province of the Roman Empire (the dress is Asiatic). No. 57, of Parian marble, is a Roman portrait statue, whose torso is first century AD with a replacement head of the third century (it was common to update statues by replacing their heads). Both statues incorporate later restorations.

THE BEAUTY ROOM

The room was devised by the 6th Duke as a tribute to the ladies of Queen Anne's court, and was used by him as a dining-room. The ducal cipher and coronet are on a carved wood panel over the Grand Staircase entrance. The Duke served the Queen as Master of the Horse (1702–11/12), while the Duchess was Groom of the Stole (1711–14). The portraits were probably inspired most directly by the set of full-lengths of 'the principal ladies attending upon her Majesty, or who were frequently in her Retinue', commissioned by the Duchess's close friend, Queen Mary, from Sir Godfrey Kneller c.1690 and known as the 'Hampton Court Beauties'. All but one of the Petworth paintings are by Michael Dahl, a Swede whom the Duke employed on other work in 1695, 1708 and 1713. The set was probably begun in 1696 and was completed by a portrait (1705) of the Duchess of Marlborough by Kneller, who also painted the portrait of the Queen. The series fortunately escaped the fire of 1714, which gutted the Grand Staircase. The 1749/50 and 1764 inventories record the portraits as in this room, with the exception of Queen Anne's portrait, which, curiously, was not listed. However, the inventories show that all bar the two overdoors were hung lower, surmounted by smaller paintings after the Italian sixteenth-century artist Polidoro da Caravaggio. Between the paintings were tall narrow bolection-moulded panels with '3 plates of Silver'd Glass in each'. The frame of the 'Pier Glass Circular Top' between the windows was part of this scheme, but it has lost its original glass 'with 4 Plates'.

According to George Jones's biography of the sculptor Sir Francis Chantrey, the Beauty Room remained unaltered until the late 1820s, when the 3rd Earl of Egremont decided to create a shrine to Napo-leon and Wellington here, hanging Jones's depictions 'of the battles of Vittoria and Waterloo, with the bust of the Duke of Wellington [1828, by Chantrey] between them'. He asked Chantrey 'about the best light for the pictures' and was told that:

the most favourable [wall] was occupied by three [in fact two] large whole-length portraits, fixed in the panels; upon which his lordship said, 'Well, I will put them there, and your bust of the Duke in the centre.' Chantrey then observed that the three portraits must in that case be removed. 'No,' said the Earl, 'I have no place for them.' 'What then is to be done?' was the natural question; to which the Earl answered, 'I will cut off their legs, I do not want their petticoats; their heads shall be placed in three small panels above, and the battles with the marble bust of the Duke shall be placed below them;' and this was done.

These alterations were already in train by 1826, including the alterations to the panelling, to Dahl's portraits and the installation of a new chimney-piece. The Beauties' legs were not in fact 'cut off', but rolled up to reduce their length. In the course of the room's restoration in 1995–6, the portraits received essential conservation treatment. Pending the longer-term possibility of restoring the paintings to full-lengths and reinstating the 6th Duke's original Beauty Room, the room has been redecorated and rehung in accordance with the 3rd Earl's Napoleonic scheme.

PAST FURNISHINGS

The Proud Duke furnished his dining-room with 'a Large Mat for dining on' and '2 Marble Side Board Tables and 1 small Oak Do' ('3 Oval Dining Tables & 2 Square Do' were stored nearby). By 1764 it was listed as the 'Beauty Room', and was simply furnished according to its new function as an ante-room between the Marble Hall and the Grand Staircase. '3 Marble Slabs with Strong Plain fraimes' supported 'Three Marble Busts', while the seat furniture still comprised the Proud Duke's 'Twelve Wallnut tree plain Chairs with flower'd Velvitt Loose Seats'. By 1869 there were four marble-topped tables, two card-tables, china vases, and a Brussels carpet and hearth rug. The curtains changed from '2 Pair of Calico Window Curtains with Cornishes' (1749/50) to 'Crimson Lute String [lustring – a crisp, plain woven silk]' (1764) to 'crimson tabaret' (1837) to 'crimson moreen [a stout woollen material]' (1869). The curtains were festoons, as are the present white damask curtains put up in 1981 (the mid-eighteenth-century pelmet boxes have been re-covered).

In 1749/50 'folding Doors' (which are known to have been 'double doors with glass above them') closed off the room from the Grand Staircase. They were removed by Salvin in the early 1870s.

FIREPLACE

The present seventeenth-century bolection-moulded marble fireplace may be the original. Certainly, it retains the 'Chimney Glass over the Chimney Piece in 3 plates with a Bolection painted Moulding' listed in 1764. However, if so, it was reintroduced after 1925, when a photograph shows a plain Neo-classical chimneypiece here in its place. This was the chimneypiece installed in 1826, presumably as part of the 3rd Earl's Napoleonic alterations.

PRINCIPAL PICTURES

Kneller's overmantel portrait of Queen Anne is in a frame supplied by Norman in 1763 at a cost of £23 2s for the copy of Holbein's portrait of Henry VIII (no. 135; Carved Room). In addition to the female portraits by Dahl, the pictures are:

NORTH WALL, OPPOSITE FIREPLACE:

LEFT AND RIGHT, LOWER REGISTER:

198, 200 GEORGE JONES, RA (1786–1869)
The Battles of Vittoria 1813 (left) *and Waterloo 1815* (right)
The pictures were commissioned by the 3rd Earl in honour of his second son, General Sir Henry Wyndham, who fought in Wellington's victories. Their hanging here prompted the alteration of the Beauty Room in the late 1820s.

CENTRE, LOWER REGISTER:

199 THOMAS PHILLIPS, RA (1770–1845)
Napoleon as First Consul
Painted from Phillips's sketch made *ad vivum* in Paris during the Peace of Amiens in 1802.

EAST WALL, OPPOSITE WINDOWS, LOWER REGISTER, FLANKING DOORWAY:

ADAM FRANS VAN DER MEULEN (1632–90)
LEFT: 203 *Louis XIV Stag-hunting at Fontainebleau*

RIGHT: 205 *Louis XIV at Maastricht*
The 3rd Earl considered these pictures of an earlier French adversary appropriate for his shrine to Napoleon – they have hung here since at least 1835.

SCULPTURE

92 SIR FRANCIS CHANTREY, RA (1781–1841)
Arthur Wellesley, 1st Duke of Wellington (1769–1852)
Signed and dated 1828.

FURNITURE

The painted high-back chairs are probably Iberian, nineteenth-century, and are part of a larger set.

BETWEEN WINDOWS:

The carved giltwood pier-table is English, *c.*1735–40; Samuel Norman added 'pieces of Foliage, Ornaments etc' in 1760 and 1762, when it stood in the Blue Drawing Room at Egremont House, Piccadilly.

PORCELAIN

ON PIER-TABLE:

The garniture of Japanese Imari porcelain is *c.*1700, and was presumably acquired by the 6th Duke of Somerset or his Duchess.

Jane, Countess of Portland; by Michael Dahl (no. 195; Beauty Room)

THE GRAND STAIRCASE

The immensely grand Grand Staircase was conceived by the 6th Duke as a palatial transition from the state apartments on the ground floor to the bedrooms upstairs. The overall concept is strongly reminiscent of Marot's design for the staircases at Het Loo and De Voorst. The murals, rich in ducal heraldry and incorporating a *Triumph of the Duchess of Somerset*, were painted by Louis Laguerre (1663–1721), one of the two foremost exponents in England of the Louis XIV style of decorative painting. By 1720, when they were completed, Laguerre's style would have seemed old-fashioned to advanced taste, but the 6th Duke was already in his late fifties and was rebuilding after a serious fire in 1714.

The fire gutted the Duke's original staircase, the foundations for which had been laid in 1691. There was a 'greate window' inserted in 1692 on the east side, with a door beneath leading into an entrance passage lit by a circular window (1692). This arrangement was repeated after 1718, except that two large windows were substituted for the single 'greate window', the door and the passageway being the principal east entrance to the house until Salvin's Victorian alterations. According to Constance Leconfield, Wilfrid Blunt said that 'it gave one such a thrill to pass from a narrow passage into the painted staircase hall, but few people were of his opinion'. The sculpture niche in the centre of the north wall was created in 1799 by blocking up an original doorway. Concurrently, a replacement door was made to the left, leading into the 3rd Earl's new Square Dining Room. The repainting demanded by filling up these doorways in the early 1870s ('by an artist named Cusius') can be clearly seen. At this stage, the present doorway at the foot of the stairs was made to give access to Salvin's new entrance hall (the Stone Hall) beyond (not open).

The balustrade of the staircase is by Charles Barry, who replaced the Duke's original arrangement around 1827 (the ropes have been copied from a 1925 photograph and are a safety measure for children). The only clue to the original treatment is an estimate headed: 'London July 23rd 1722 Proposal of John Simmons Joyner for the Great Staircase. 29 steps (3 half paces perquetr'd with two banesters on each step (as before)'. This suggests that part of the floor was inlaid with parquetry, and

the floor as it is now may be essentially the early eighteenth-century structure.

In 1814 a section of marble flooring was installed as the plinth for a stove, perhaps for the visit of the Allied Sovereigns that year; the staircase must have been extremely cold beforehand. This stood in the centre of the wall under the stairs and was still in place in 1869, when it was protected by a 'High wire guard'.

PAST FURNISHINGS

The 1749/50 and 1764 inventories list the same light fittings: 'Nine Gilt Square Lanthorns', which may have been fixed to the newel posts, as their late Victorian successors are today, and 'Two Hexigon Lanthorns hung with gilt Iron Chains under the Landing'. Otherwise, in 1764 there were no fewer than four card-tables (presumably placed here until needed elsewhere) and 'Two Mahogany 3 Leav'd Dumb Waiters'.

By 1867 there were two marble-topped tables (probably those made in 1814, one of which had a black and gold frame), a Brussels carpet and four of the black and gold hall-chairs still here.

In 1823 Thomas Phillips's equestrian portrait of the Prince Regent of 1813 (no. 587) was hung across the double doors at the centre of the upstairs landing. Turner depicted it here in the late 1820s, where it remained until c.1870 and where it has been temporarily reinstated.

WALL-PAINTINGS

This is one of Laguerre's last painted schemes (1718–20), for which he received £200 in 1720. It was painted at the same time as his masterpiece, the Saloon at Blenheim. The principal theme is the story of Prometheus and Pandora. In Classical mythology, Prometheus stole fire from the gods, and was punished by Jupiter who chained him to a rock. He was released by Hercules. According to Ovid's *Metamorphoses* (i, 76–88), he fashioned man from clay (a scene depicted in the lower staircase hall). Jupiter punished mankind for Prometheus's theft of fire by making Pandora open her box (depicted on the ceiling), which unleashed all the world's evils. Only hope remained inside. The story is depicted in general terms, but the choice of subject must be an allusion to the disastrous fire of 1714.

SCULPTURE

IN NICHE:

128 *Marble bust of ? William III*
by Honoré Pelle
Pelle was a Provençal who worked in Genoa
and Modena before coming to England. He was
inspired by Bernini's bust of Louis XIV (1665;
Versailles) in creating this truly Baroque image of
kingship. This bust is probably the 'marble head
representing the late King William' for which
the Duke paid £6 in 1724. However, the nose is a
replacement so it may be a portrait of James II.

CENTRE OF ROOM:

88 *Silenus nursing the Infant Bacchus*, an eighteenth
or early nineteenth-century bronze copy of the
Imperial Roman marble statue (Louvre, Paris),
discovered in Rome *c.*1569, and purchased in 1807
by Napoleon from the Villa Borghese, Rome. This
copy, bought by the 3rd Earl, stood in 1835 at the
centre of the South Corridor of the North Gallery.

FURNITURE

BENEATH NICHE:

The black and gold table is probably Florentine,
*c.*1690, and is one of five mentioned in the 1749/50
inventory belonging to the Proud Duke, and is
probably in the most original condition.

UNDER STAIRS:

The pair of carved giltwood candlestands is English,
*c.*1760, and was probably supplied by Samuel
Norman, probably for Egremont House, London.

AROUND LOWER HALL:

The black and gold sgabello hall-chairs are English
or Italian, *c.*1615–35. There are two sets of nine,
one set bearing the Percy crescent beneath an
Earl's coronet in the centre of the splat. They
could have been made for either the 9th or 10th Earls
of Northumberland, both of whom visited Italy.
(The 10th Earl purchased 'backstooles of the Italian
fashion' in 1635–6.) They were originally unpainted
(the wood is walnut) and gilt. In 1680 they stood in
the 'lobby' at Petworth where they were described
as 'eighteen carved and gilt wood [chairs] with halfe
moons'. In 1749/50 the whole set was in the Marble
Hall. They may have been painted black before 1764,
when 'Twelve Black & Gilt hall Chairs' stood in an
adjoining vestibule. Such chairs are extremely rare.

AROUND ROOM:

The lacquer chests on stands are late seventeenth-
century Chinese or Japanese on Anglo-Dutch
late seventeenth-century ebonised supports. They
were traditionally decorated with garnitures of
oriental porcelain jars.

The carved walnut stands for porcelain jars are
English, *c.*1690, and are extremely rare survivals
of stands specifically designed to support weighty
pieces of porcelain of the type displayed here.
The Petworth stands, of four different patterns
(some are in the Carved Room, see p. 30), were
made for the Duchess of Somerset who, like her
friend Queen Mary, was bitten by the china-
mania that swept through the northern courts in
the late seventeenth century. Such stands survive
only at Petworth and at Hampton Court.

PORCELAIN

The blue-and-white porcelain jars, here and elsewhere,
are Chinese, Kangxi period (1662–1722) and were
purchased by the 6th Duke and Duchess.

CARPET

IN LOWER HALL:

The woollen carpet with woven inscription 'EXON
1758' was made at the Exeter factory of Claude
Passavant (d.1766). This is one of only three dated
examples of this type based on designs by Pierre-
Josse Perrot, the principal carpet designer of the
Savonnerie (*c.*1724–50).

The Grand Staircase

The Little Dining Room

raits by Lely as overdoors, while Ramsay's state portrait of George III (Mrs Wyndham's Bedroom) was over the fireplace. The 1764 inventory also indicates that the room was intended by the 2nd Earl of Egremont for the display of Antique statuary. There were no fewer than 'Six Marble terms of Different Sort of Marble and six Marble Busts on D°' (these marble plinths are now mainly in the North Gallery). The sculptural theme was continued by the 3rd Earl, who in 1813 installed the wooden plinths for full-length Antique statues in the corners of the room.

Turner's sketch of this room (*c*.1827) reveals that it was probably painted red and shows an orchestra playing here during a banquet in the Carved Room next door. On such occasions the Little Dining Room was used as a servery. In 1869 the room was a sitting-room and was subsequently redecorated by the 2nd Lord Leconfield with a red flock wallpaper. This must have been hung on battens over the panelling and was bordered by a gilt fillet, but no trace of it remains. However, the faded blue and salmon pink curtains may still survive from this scheme. Their pattern, in stamped velvet, would have complemented a damask flock paper. They replaced the crimson silk festoon curtains listed in 1869, which may have been survivals from the 2nd Earl's day (identical curtains were listed in 1764), The present pale blue and white decoration was commissioned by the Trust from John Fowler in the early 1950s.

THE LITTLE DINING ROOM

In 1749/50 it was called 'The Red Leather Chair Room' after its '12 Stuff'd Back & Seat Chairs of Red Leather with brass Nails' (still here in 1764). It then had a corner fireplace (to the left of the present one) with shelves above for ornamental porcelain. By 1764 it was known as the Oak Room, probably because of the panelling, which was then presumably unpainted and dates from the 1690s (the 6th Duke's arms and coronet can be seen in the delicately carved woodwork of the cornice). In 1764 there were eight Van Dycks here, and this concentration of his portraiture survived well into the nineteenth century when it was called the 'Vandyke Room', and has recently been restored. In 1764 there were also two port-

PRINCIPAL PICTURES

WALL OPPOSITE FIREPLACE, BELOW LEFT:

220 SIR ANTHONY VAN DYCK (1599–1641)
Lady Dorothy Percy, Countess of Leicester (1598–1659)
The eldest daughter of the 9th Earl of Northumberland, sister of the 10th Earl, and the mother of Lady Dorothy Sidney, Countess of Sunderland (1617–84), who was celebrated in the poems of Edmund Waller as 'Sacharissa'. This, and the other female portraits by Van Dyck here (nos. 288, 245) and in the White and Gold Room, are part of a group put together by the 10th Earl, who was emulating the continental fashion for portrait series of beautiful and famous women.

295 SIR ANTHONY VAN DYCK (1599–1641)
Katherine Bruce, Mrs William Murray (d.1649)

The redoubtable wife of William Murray, later 1st Earl of Dysart, who was a childhood friend of Charles I and shared his artistic interests. Part of the 1st Earl's collection survives at Ham House, Richmond (National Trust). He would have known the 10th Earl of Northumberland, and this may explain the presence at Petworth of this portrait, which was listed at Northumberland House in 1671.

WALL OPPOSITE WINDOWS:

288 Sir ANTHONY VAN DYCK (1599–1641)
Anne Boteler, Countess of Newport (*c*.1605/10–69)
She was married in 1626/7 to Mountjoy Blount, created 1st Earl of Newport in 1628, the left-hand figure in the Van Dyck double portrait in the Square Dining Room (no. 300).

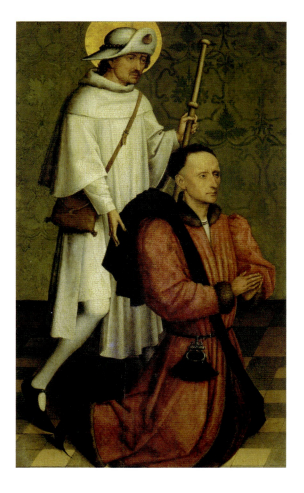

OVER DOOR:

342 SIMON VERELST (1644–1710)
Prince Rupert of the Rhine (1619–82)
The son of Charles I's sister, Elizabeth, Queen of Bohemia ('The Winter Queen'), and a dashing royalist cavalry commander in the Civil War. The elaborate frame was probably made for the 6th Duke in the 1680s or 1690s.

OVER CHIMNEYPIECE:

Around the large central painting are groups of fifteenth- and sixteenth-century French, Flemish, German and Netherlandish paintings, including (nos. 122A and B) *The Virgin Annunciate* and *St James and a Donor*, two fragments attributed to Rogier van der Weyden (1399–1464); and two male portraits (nos. 175 and 322) by Joos van Cleve (active 1511–40/1).

601 GERARD SEGHERS (1591–1651)
St Sebastian
A late work by this Antwerp artist painted under the influence of Van Dyck. Purchased by the 10th Earl of Northumberland. The carved frame is exceptional for retaining its original black and silver decoration of *c*.1660.

St James and a Donor; attributed to Rogier van der Weyden (no. 122; Little Dining Room)

25

FURNITURE

BETWEEN WINDOWS:

The pier-glass in chinoiserie style is one of the group supplied by Whittle and Norman in the 1750s and early 1760s.

OPPOSITE FIREPLACE:

The giltwood side-table is English, *c.*1735.

OPPOSITE WINDOWS:

The pair of side-tables is English, *c.*1710, and was repainted in the early 1950s, having originally been 'white painted', according to the 1837 inventory.

The lacquer cabinets on stands are Japanese, seventeenth-century, on ebonised Anglo-Dutch late seventeenth-century stands.

PORCELAIN

ON TABLE OPPOSITE FIREPLACE:

*Dishes from a Meissen dessert service, c.*1735-40 (marked), in hard-paste porcelain painted in enamels in the Japanese kakiemon style, named after Sakaida Kakiemon (1596–1666), who is credited with introducing to Japan in 1644 the process of painting in overglaze enamel colours on a milk-white ground. The style was widely imitated in Europe in the early eighteenth century.

ON TABLES FLANKING DOORWAY OPPOSITE WINDOWS:

*Part of a Meissen service, c.*1770 (marked), with floral decoration painted in enamels. Probably acquired by the 3rd Earl on his Grand Tour in 1770, when he visited Meissen and spent £55 2s on china.

CHANDELIER

The ormolu and cut-glass chandelier, the corona formed of intertwined snakes, is one of a pair, *c.*1820. They were hanging in the Marble Hall by *c.*1865, when they were depicted in Mrs Wyndham's watercolour.

THE CARVED ROOM

The first Carved Room was half its present size. It was constructed around 1690 by Grinling Gibbons, who produced 'the most superb monument of his skill' (in Horace Walpole's words) for the 6th Duke of Somerset. Gibbons's room occupied the southern half of the present room (the visitor enters it from the south) and, as the 1749/50 and 1764 inventories reveal, incorporated the two pairs of full-length portraits (now at either end of the long fireplace wall) 'flounced all about with carving', four other 'Pictures of full Length in carv'd frames' and three half-lengths over the doors. In 1786 the 3rd Earl began the process (completed in 1792–4) of doubling the size of the room. He removed the partition wall and brought in late seventeenth-century carvings from elsewhere in the house. The elaborate carvings and frame around the portrait of Henry VIII after Holbein were probably carved in 1689–90 by John Selden for the Proud Duke's Dining Room.

Gibbons and Selden intended their limewood carvings to be seen as lighter in tone than the oak panelling to which they are pinned. However, the 3rd Earl had the panelling painted white so that the carvings appeared darker than their background. The white paint was stripped from the panelling in 1872, but the effect can still be appreciated in the cove and ceiling. Between 1828 and 1846 the 3rd Earl's carver, Jonathan Ritson, added numerous carvings in Gibbons's style to the walls and ceiling. These accretions were also removed in 1870–2, and in the process, four landscapes by Turner, painted for the room in the late 1820s were removed from the panelling beneath the four full-length portraits on the principal fireplace wall. In 2000–2, Ritson's carvings, Turner's landscapes and other elements of the 3rd Earl's scheme were restored to the Carved Room.

THE ORIGINAL CARVED ROOM

'A bill paid to Mr Gibbons for Carving ... £150' on 10 December 1692 suggests that work was already far advanced. According to the 1749/50 inventory, which called it the 'carved Room', Van Dyck's equestrian portrait of Charles I hung over the single chimneypiece on the east wall (it is now the overmantel at the far [north] end of the room). There were only three overdoor

The Carved Room following restoration of the 3rd Earl's arrangement in 2000–2

portraits by Lely (rather than four as at present) and this reflects a nearly contemporary ground plan incorporated in Laguerre's staircase paintings, which shows two doors on the principal enfilade and a third door (now blocked up) leading from the right-hand corner of the long fireplace wall into the Oak Staircase. Otherwise, we know that the room contained in all '8 Pictures at full length in carv'd frames' and 'Three Peer glass fraimes Carv'd in Lime Tree with 2 plates in Each', on the window wall.

This smaller room would have given greater prominence to Gibbons's delicately carved crestings and festoons surrounding the four full-length portraits of the Duke and Duchess of Somerset and of the Duke's grandparents, originally placed on the north and south walls respectively, so that they were lit from the side. Their carved frames, incorporating the Duke's winged crest, his Garter and other armorials, represent the summit of Gibbons's achievement as the designer and executor of grand décor. In 1749 Horace Walpole enthused: 'There are birds, absolutely feathered, and two antique vases with bas relieves as perfect and beautiful as if they were carved by some Grecian master.'

THE 3RD EARL'S CARVED ROOM

The early nineteenth century saw a revival of interest in Gibbons, and the 3rd Earl's Carved Room was intended to do honour to him and his school. The originally light-coloured limewood carvings would already have darkened by 1814, when the 'mouldings and wainscot' were repaired 'for painting', and 'whitewashing' with lime-wash was undertaken to lighten the carvings.

The carvings were then displayed on a lighter (warm white) ground, thus reversing the original concept of the carvings as light accents on darker panels. In 1833 W. G. Rogers, a notable restorer of wood carvings, was 'pained' by the 'meagre' appearance of 'the dirty washed wood on the white walls'.

C. R. Leslie's view of the north-west corner, painted c.1828 (Tate), shows an Antique bust (one of four) placed between windows hung with scarlet festoon curtains. Subsequently, Jonathan Ritson single-handedly added carvings to the ceiling and covered every available space on the walls with 'drops' in Gibbonsesque style. The results of his labours can be seen in Mrs Wyndham's depiction of the room in about 1865. Ritson was 'discovered' by the 3rd Earl through his work at Arundel Castle for the Duke of Norfolk. From 1828, he was paid an average of £60 per annum, and his work in the Carved Room was finished 'only a week before he died' in 1846. The 3rd Earl thought highly enough of his work to commission his portrait by Clint,

which still hangs here as a pendant to Clint's portrait of Gibbons. Ritson's life was one of intermittent industry and drunkenness: 'his only pleasures were his works and his cups', wrote a contemporary. Most of Ritson's carving was dismantled in 1870–2 and was mainly in store until the restoration of the 3rd Earl's scheme for the Carved Room in 2000–2.

The 3rd Earl's Carved Room was conceived as a dining-room large enough for banquets. Mrs Wyndham thought the room 'very pleasant and comfortable even for a small party', and it was used for dining until well into the present century. It was also a setting for royal and family portraits (the 3rd Earl's mother and sisters were added to the Seymour full-lengths), for Antique statuary, blue-and-white Chinese porcelain, and by the late 1820s and early 1830s for four of Turner's landscapes, as well as Shakespearean scenes by Clint and Leslie. In August 1828 Thomas Creevey noted that three landscapes by Turner were already installed. At least two of these came from the trial set of landscapes for the Carved Room (Tate), and were

The Carved Room, c.1865, watercolour-gouache by the Hon. Mrs. Percy. (Madeline) Wyndham (Carved Room)

replaced by the more finished set still at Petworth. The final change was probably made in 1830, when the estate accounts (for 25 September) read: 'taking down carved picture frames, taking out and putting in pictures and fixing them again in the long dining room'. The frames were by Ritson, who supplied the similar frames around the smaller pictures still hanging in the room. It is extraordinary that Turner's landscapes were hung beneath the full-length ancestral portraits on the main wall, and that they formed part of a decorative and dynastic scheme which must have been the 3rd Earl's own conception.

Unhappily, however, Lord and Lady Lecon-field dismantled the 3rd Earl's arrangement in 1870–2, and, in the process, the tangible evidence of one of Turner's most exceptional commissions. The National Trust has undertaken its restoration (2000–2) as part of the essential conservation of the Carved Room's woodwork, which has also been completed thanks to a generous donation.

PICTURES

EAST WALL, LEFT AND RIGHT:

GEORGE CLINT, ARA (1770–1854)
147* *Grinling Gibbons* (1648–1721)
147** *Jonathan Ritson* (c.1780–1846)
These portraits of the craftsmen who created the carvings here were commissioned by the 3rd Earl for the room. The carved frames are by Ritson.

125, 126, 145, 147 *The overdoors* are by Sir PETER LELY (1618–80).

AT FAR, NORTH END:

124 Sir ANTHONY VAN DYCK (1599–1641) and others
King Charles I on horseback
Left unfinished in Van Dyck's studio on his death, it was acquired by the 10th Earl of Northumberland and is described at Northumberland House in 1671 with the note: 'the face not finished'. This portrait was placed over the single fireplace in Gibbons's original Carved Room.

AT SOUTH END:

146 After Sir ANTHONY VAN DYCK (1599–1641)
Queen Henrietta Maria (1609–69) and her Dwarf, Jeffery Hudson (1619–82)
Charles I's consort took Hudson into her service after he leapt from a pie at a dinner given by the Duchess of Buckingham.

LONG, PRINCIPAL WALL, OPPOSITE WINDOWS:

UPPER REGISTER:

131, 133, 166, 143 The four portraits of the 3rd Earl's relations are by THOMAS PHILLIPS, RA (1770–1845); no. 131 is after JEAN-ETIENNE LIOTARD (1702–89) and nos. 166 and 143 after Sir JOSHUA REYNOLDS, PRA (1723–92)

LOWER REGISTER:

144, 138, 128, 134 The first three Shakespearean scenes are by GEORGE CLINT, ARA (1770–1854); the fourth is by CHARLES ROBERT LESLIE, RA (1794–1859)

LEFT OF FIREPLACE, ABOVE:

129, 127 JOHN CLOSTERMAN (c.1660–1711)
The 6th Duke (1662–1748), 1692, and Duchess of Somerset (1667–1722)
The Duke was Gibbons's patron both at Petworth and at Trinity College, Cambridge. The Duchess is depicted with a son, presumably her eldest son, the 7th Duke (1684–1750).

LEFT OF FIREPLACE, BELOW:

130 J. M. W. TURNER, RA (1775–1851)
Chichester Canal, c.1828–30
The Portsmouth & Arundel Canal lost the 3rd Earl at least £55,000 and was unprofitable after its completion in 1823. Lord Egremont withdrew from the company in 1826, but still commissioned this.

132 J. M. W. TURNER, RA (1775–1851)
Petworth Park, c.1828–30
A suitably idyllic vision of the park created by 'Capability' Brown, with a cricket match in progress and deer wandering up to the windows of the west front, as they still can.

OVER FIREPLACE:

135 After HANS HOLBEIN the Younger (1497/8–1543)
King Henry VIII (1491–1547)
Derived from the dynastic fresco painted in the Privy Chamber of Whitehall Palace in 1537 and destroyed by fire in 1698. This version was painted in Holbein's studio. The pastiche portrait of Anne Boleyn (also after Holbein) is c.1830.

RIGHT OF FIREPLACE, ABOVE:

141, 139 These two early seventeenth-century full-lengths of the 6th Duke of Somerset's grandfather, *The 1st Lord Seymour of Trowbridge*

The Carved Room looking North by C. R. Leslie, c.1828 (Tate)

(?1590–1664) and an unknown woman called 'Lady Seymour' by WILLIAM LARKIN (active c.1609–d.1619) were on the south wall of Gibbons's original smaller Carved Room, facing Closterman's portraits of the 6th Duke and Duchess.

RIGHT OF FIREPLACE, BELOW:

140 J. M. W. TURNER, RA (1775–1851)
Brighton from the Sea, c.1828–30

142 J. M. W. TURNER, RA (1775–1851)
The Lake in Petworth Park, c.1828–30

FURNITURE

WINDOW WALL:

The pair of carved giltwood pier-tables with 'bianco e nero' (black and white) marble and ormolu tops is Italian, *c.*1750, possibly with additions by Samuel Norman (the carved aprons seem more English than Italian). There is a long drawer at the back of each table, probably for the storage of maps, scrolls or even swords. They are probably the 'bianco e nero'

tables supplied in 1760 for Egremont House, Piccadilly, by 'Mr Wilton' – probably Joseph Wilton, RA (1722–1803).

CENTRE:

The elaborate giltwood side-table with the porphyry top incorporating the cross of Lorraine in the legs is French, Louis XIV, *c.*1700, and was presumably made for a member of the House of Lorraine.

NORTH END, FIREPLACE WALL, ON NORTH CHIMNEYPIECE:

89a ROBERT HENDERSON (active 1820–32)
Whalebone
This bronze statuette of one of the 3rd Earl's racehorses appears in Phillips's portrait of him (no. 695; North Gallery).

PRINCIPAL FIREPLACE WALL, OPPOSITE WINDOWS:

The walnut pedestals for porcelain jars are *c.*1690 and were made for the 6th Duke and Duchess of Somerset (see p. 72).

The carved walnut armchairs (also on end walls) upholstered with tapestry are English in the Louis XV style, *c.*1760, and were probably supplied by Paul Saunders (1722–71) of Soho Square, London, whose 1763 bill to the 2nd Earl of Egremont's executors mentions 'French Elbow Chairs'. Saunders was a prominent upholsterer, who made tapestry as well as furniture, and in 1757 he was appointed 'Tapestry Maker to His Majesty'. He supplied tapestries after designs by Zuccarelli for Egremont House, which were largely completed in 1760, and the tapestry covers of these armchairs are illustrations from Aesop's *Fables*, a 1666 edition of which, illustrated by Francis Barlow, was frequently used as a basis for upholstery.

FLANKING FIREPLACE:

The pair of marble tables on giltwood supports is English, *c.*1735. The porphyry tops are edged in green marble and banded with ormolu.

ON SOUTH CHIMNEYPIECE:

The ormolu-mounted Boulle bracket clock probably dates from the *Régence* period (1715–23), the first phase of the French Rococo. Inscribed 'Minoche à Paris' – probably Jean Minoche.

INSIDE PRINCIPAL FIREPLACE:

The fireback is dated 1622 and bears the coronet,

crescent device and initials of the 9th Earl of Northumberland, who was released from the Tower in 1621.

The andirons surmounted by sixteenth-century North European statuettes are the larger of two sets of 'Iron Doges', one 'with a Statue on Each', listed in 1764. 'Two large figured An[d]irons' were purchased by the 6th Duke in 1689.

CHANDELIERS

The two pairs of ormolu chandeliers are French, late eighteenth- or early nineteenth-century, in the style of the *Régence* period (1715–23), and were presumably acquired for the room by the 3rd Earl after 1793–4, when he completed its extension.

The Red Room; watercolour-gouache by J. M. W. Turner, c.1827 (Tate)

CARPET

The carpet is possibly Irish, Donegal, early twentieth-century.

THE RED ROOM
(formerly the Turner Room)

In the Proud Duke's time, this was the 'Picture Room next to ye North Cloisters', containing no fewer than '60 Pictures of different sizes'. Called the Green Drawing Room in the 1764 inventory, it was redecorated by the 3rd Earl in 1806, when it was described as 'the new Crimson Room by the North Gallery'. In 1952, when Anthony Blunt collected together here almost all the twenty paintings by Turner in the collection, it was hung with yellow silk and became known as the Turner Room. Its previous name has recently been readopted, given the reversion to the 3rd Earl's décor, which is recorded in paintings by both Turner and Leslie.

Both views also show Van Dyck's full-length portraits of Sir Robert and Lady Shirley (already here in 1764) hanging either side of the North Gallery door. This arrangement has been restored, as has the pattern of adjacent pictures depicted by Turner. Both Turner's and Leslie's views show that the room had a dark skirting board, white woodwork and that it retained the blue-and-white Chinese jars and Antique sculpture listed in 1764. Leslie's painting indicates that there was a red festoon *portière* curtain in the Red Room above the doorway leading from the Carved Room and this presumably matched the window curtains. The building accounts record that the crimson walls were bordered by a gilt moulding put up in 1806.

PAST FURNISHINGS

The Proud Duke had sixteen chairs upholstered with 'blue velvet bound with gold lace', which were still here in 1764, when they were described as having 'very high Backs Cover'd with flower'd Velvett & Silk Tassells fring Cover'd Backs & Seats with Blue Loose Covers'. Apart from the Shirley Van Dycks, there were seven pictures in 1764 (all portraits) including (as overmantel) the copy of Holbein's portrait of Henry VIII (moved by the 3rd Earl into the Carved Room and still there). By 1835 there was a catholic mix of 30 pictures, both portraits and landscapes, including Rembrandt's *Lady with a Fan*, sold in 1927 and now in the Metropolitan Museum, New York. The room may have had an occasional use as a dining-room in the mid-nineteenth century, judging by the presence in 1869 of a 'Mahog. telescope dining table'.

At some stage after 1869 (probably in the early 1870s) the 2nd Lord Leconfield commissioned Morris & Co. to redecorate the room. Morris's festoon curtains survive (gold silk faded to brown, in 'Larkspur' pattern) and the walls were silked to match. At some stage between 1925 and 1952, when Anthony Blunt replaced 'the horrid crimson wall-coverings' with yellow silk (chosen by the Dowager Lady Egremont), the room must have reverted to red.

CHIMNEYPIECE

The 3rd Earl installed a new chimneypiece in 1832 (probably plain marble similar to those in the North Gallery). The present late seventeenth-century carved chimneypiece had been 'lying by in an attic', before it was placed here by the 2nd Lord Leconfield, probably in the early 1870s concurrently with the room's redecoration by Morris & Co.

PRINCIPAL PICTURES

SOUTH, ENTRANCE WALL:

LEFT OF DOORWAY, BELOW:

665 J. M. W. TURNER, RA (1775–1851)
The Confluence of the Thames and the Medway,
exh. 1808

RIGHT OF DOORWAY, ABOVE:

590 UNKNOWN NETHERLANDISH PAINTER, 1602
Henry Percy, 9th Earl of Northumberland
(1564–1632)
The inscription states that this somewhat bizarre and provincial portrait was 'drawne in the loe Contries 1602', where the Wizard Earl was on

Teresia, Lady Shirley; by Sir Anthony van Dyck, 1622 (no. 97; Red Room)

campaign. He and other noble volunteers were criticised by their commander for the extravagance of their dress and retinues.

BELOW:

672 J. M. W. TURNER, RA (1775–1851)
Margate, exhibited 1808

NORTH WALL, EITHER SIDE OF DOOR INTO NORTH GALLERY:

LEFT ABOVE:

96 Sir ANTHONY VAN DYCK (1599–1641)
Sir Robert Shirley (?1581–1628)
This magnificent portrait and its companion (no. 97) were probably painted in Rome in 1622, while Shirley was on a diplomatic mission as Persian Ambassador from Shah Abbas the Great of Persia to Pope Gregory XV. They were probably purchased by the 2nd Earl and are first listed at Petworth in 1764.

RIGHT, ABOVE:

97 Sir ANTHONY VAN DYCK (1599–1641)
Teresia, Lady Shirley (d.1668)
A Circassian Christian noblewoman, wife of Sir Robert Shirley (no. 96).

RIGHT, BELOW:

48 ANTOINE, LOUIS (both active 1629–48) and MATHIEU LE NAIN (c.1607–77)
A Peasant Family
The Le Nain brothers are best known for such unsentimental 'low-life' scenes. Painted in 1642, according to records of a now vanished date and signature, and inherited by the 3rd Earl from his uncle, the Earl of Thomond, in 1774.

SCULPTURE

ON PIER-TABLE, BETWEEN WINDOWS:

73 *Head of Aphrodite, the 'Leconfield Aphrodite'*, Parian marble, Greek, fourth century BC, attributed to Praxiteles, one of the greatest of Greek sculptors. Originally the head of a full-length statue of Aphrodite (Venus), and bought from Gavin Hamilton in 1755. The groove across the top of the head probably held a bronze fillet; the nose and upper lip have been restored and the surface has been repolished by a mid-eighteenth-century restorer, possibly Bartolomeo Cavaceppi (1716–99).

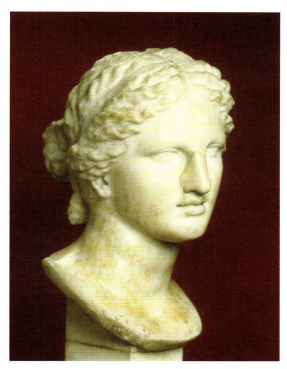

The 'Leconfield Aphrodite'; attributed to Praxiteles (no. 73; Red Room)

FURNITURE

BETWEEN WINDOWS:

The giltwood pier-glass, c.1755–60, is the largest and most exotic of the magnificent group attributable to Whittle and Norman. *The pier-table* is Italian, c.1700–25.

SOUTH EAST CORNER:

The sarcophagus-shaped commode of black Boulle-work with superb ormolu mounts, including terminal winged sphinxes and lion's paw feet is French, c.1710, by the famous *ébéniste* André-Charles Boulle. Two commodes at Versailles are virtually identical and are the only surviving pieces of furniture known to have been made by Boulle himself (for the Grand Trianon in 1708–9). This commode, the *bureau plat* to the right of the North Gallery door, and two clocks (pp. 14 and 30) were purchased by the 2nd Lord Leconfield from the London dealer Colnaghi, after the legendary Hamilton

Palace sale in 1882, where this commode (lot 994) fetched the then enormous sum of £1,081 10s.

THE NORTH GALLERY

HISTORY

The North Gallery is one of the very few top-lit sculpture and picture galleries to survive from the early nineteenth century. It was extensively restored in 1991–3. The gallery is divided into three main spaces. The visitor first enters the South Corridor, the earliest part of the gallery, which was built between 1754 and 1763 to house the major part of the 2nd Earl's collection of Antique statuary. This was formed by Matthew Brettingham the Elder from an open cloister (the medieval chapel is nearby), and was lit by tall round-headed sash-windows, which were fitted into the cloister arches. Four of these window openings can still be seen and now look through to the present Central Corridor, which was added to his father's gallery by the 3rd Earl in 1824–5.

Although the 2nd Earl's sculpture gallery has therefore been considerably altered (the side windows in the South Corridor are other nineteenth-century alterations), it retains many of the original elements described in the 1764 inventory. Eight of the original nine niches for full-length statues can still be seen on the south wall, and the 'Six Marble Busts in the Oval Recesses on Plaister Brackets on the window Side of the Room' are still in place on the north wall. The marble statues in the niches are in the sequence recorded in 1835. In 1764 there were also two statues 'Sitting in the Nitches at the End upon Wood Pedistals' and six marble busts 'on Plaister Brackets in the Bow' (there was a bay window in the north wall). The gallery was sparsely furnished with 'Eight Japand Bamboo Chairs with Cane Bottoms and Crimson Moreen Cushions' and a 'Mahogany turn over Table'.

Thus the gallery remained until 1824, apart from various minor alterations including the provision of brackets and wooden plinths for additional statuary. Judging by the building accounts, the gallery appears to have remained a statue gallery *per se*; there is no mention of pictures being hung. It was regularly used for large dinners, and tables were put up and taken down as required for the entertainment of the tenantry or the 'cavalry' (the

local yeomanry). However, by 1824 the 3rd Earl needed more space for his ever-increasing collection and the present top-lit Central Corridor was completed at the end of 1825. Immediately, work began on the final extension (the Square Bay) and the whole was finished in October 1827. The works were supervised by Thomas Upton, the Petworth Clerk of Works, and executed by his building yard. Upton apparently acted without the direction of an architect, and it is probable that the 3rd Earl had much to say about the design. He is known to have sought the advice of at least three artists: the painter Thomas Phillips and the sculptors Sir Francis Chantrey and John Edward Carew.

The Petworth gallery is strongly reminiscent of several earlier London galleries, most notably Sir John Soane's Dulwich Picture Gallery (1811–15), the first public gallery in England. Both have wide arched openings, simple detailing and top-lighting. Neither has a dado, allowing for pictures to be hung as low as required, and to be crammed in thickly between cornice and floor. It is possible that the *éminence grise* behind the design of the Petworth gallery was Soane, who was consulted on other Petworth schemes by Lord Egremont in 1814 and 1816.

DECORATION

The walls of Brettingham's sculpture gallery (the present South Corridor) were painted grey-blue. Following the 3rd Earl's extensions, the gallery was painted white (as Turner depicted it in *c*.1827) with a dark skirting. Paint analysis has established that it was a bright cool white. White was a fashionable colour for sculpture galleries at this date, but, as at the British Museum, it was found to show up the dirtiness of Antique sculpture, and this may explain why the gallery was painted a browny red. Red (with green, the most traditional colour for picture galleries) was felt by Ruskin to accentuate the contours of sculpture, and it was known to have been used in ancient Rome as a foil to sculpture. The change may have been made in the 3rd Earl's lifetime, although the vignette of the gallery in Phillips's full-length posthumous portrait of the Earl (1839) still shows the gallery painted white. By *c*.1865, the date of Madeline Wyndham's water-colour view, the gallery was a light red with the spandrels of the arches picked out in blue (paint analysis has failed to detect the blue). In 1873, during Salvin's alterations to Petworth, a darker red

The North Gallery, c.1827, when the walls were white;
watercolour-gouache by J. M. W. Turner (Tate)

was adopted. The oil-painted walls were varnished to give a glossy appearance, the cornice was painted in brown, black and terracotta in the manner of Antique Greek pottery, and the skirting boards were painted black.

By 1925, the gallery had been repainted in green, woodchip paper was applied in *c.*1936, and finally in the early 1950s, the Trust commissioned John Fowler to redecorate in pinky terracotta on the basis of a section of old paint found in the gallery. As part of the restoration in 1991–3, Fowler's scheme was removed, and the 1873 dark red decoration was uncovered and patched where missing; the original varnish had lost its sheen and was not renewed. The result promotes the impression that the gallery has survived unaltered since the nineteenth century.

CHIMNEYPIECES

The original grey marble chimneypieces (of 1824 and 1827) have been recovered from store and replaced in their original positions (in the Central Corridor and Square Bay). They had been removed after 1925. Central-heating pipework (which ran beneath the pictures and was extremely harmful to them) was installed probably at the beginning of this century and has now been replaced by an underfloor convection-heating system disguised by newly acquired Victorian cast-iron grilles which maintains the relative humidity at a conservation level. Originally, the open fires were supplemented by stoves (in 1826) and a 'hot water apparatus' (1830), of which no trace remains. It was recognised that heating was essential not only for comfort but to maintain the pictures and sculpture in a satisfactory state.

The Central Corridor in the North Gallery c.1865; watercolour-gouache by the Hon. Mrs Percy (Madeline) Wyndham (no. 706; North Gallery)

SEAT FURNITURE

As early as Turner's view of the gallery (c.1827), seats were placed in the gallery for the ease of visitors – 'chair and sofa furniture' was changed in 1835 and 1836. The large red sofa shown by Turner does not survive, but the set of mid-nineteenth-century upholstered sofas on turned oak supports has been renovated and re-covered. Some had been specially designed to be placed next to sculpture plinths.

CARPETS

The original furnishings included carpets, of which no trace survives. The new carpets (1997) are copies of the carpets laid c.1870 in the Picture Gallery at Attingham Park, Shropshire.

LIGHTING

The 3rd Earl's advisers took great pains to ensure that the top-lighting of the gallery was effective. Originally in 1824, the skylights had sloping sides, but the present upright design was adopted in 1839 for the Square Bay, a pattern copied for the Central Corridor in 1843. This, according to Phillips, was 'to bring the light nearer to the pictures' and was devised by reference to the skylights at the Royal Academy. The skylights were recently rebuilt to the original design. Blinds, controlled by ropes from the floor, limited light damage and at least two pictures were provided with protective curtains (in 1836), presumably for the same reason. At night, three colza oil lanterns (in the much darker South Corridor) provided illumination (two of these survive elsewhere in the house) and a gas lantern was placed in the centre of the Central Corridor; gas pipes (installed in 1843) were discovered in the course of the recent restoration. Gas lighting was eventually replaced by electricity. The early twentieth-century brass electroliers, in seventeenth-century style, are still in place. Recently, picture lights have been introduced (to the pre-1925 Petworth design) in the South Corridor.

PICTURES

HANG

Turner's view of *c*.1827 shows that pictures were already hung above the niches in the South Corridor (the 2nd Earl's sculpture gallery). Turner also depicts Owen's portrait of *Mrs Robinson* (no. 13) over the chimneypiece in the Square Bay (it now hangs opposite). There is no other visual record of the gallery in the 3rd Earl's day, and the earliest evidence within his lifetime is H. W. Phillips's list of pictures in 1835. This reveals that, apart from 24 Old Masters, the remaining 67 pictures were by British or American artists. Soon after the 3rd Earl's death, probably between 1839 and 1842, record diagrams of the picture-hang were drawn. These (and Mrs Wyndham's *c*.1865 watercolour of the gallery) have been used as the principal sources of information for the rehanging of the gallery along historical lines. Pictures have now once again been hung above the sculpture niches as depicted by Turner. Two pairs of Turner landscapes hang at either end of the Central Corridor, somewhat uncomfortably jammed into the available space, but exactly as recorded soon after the 3rd Earl's death.

The brass picture rail probably dates from 1873 and was certainly in place by 1925. Picture rails were in use at least as early as the seventeenth century, to allow maximum flexibility for the display of pictures. It is much easier to move a picture supported by chains, as there is no need to renew the wall fixings, but although the 3rd Earl's pictures were in a continual state of flux, they were fixed individually, (as recorded in 1825). Neither Turner nor Mrs Wyndham show a picture rail.

SOUTH CORRIDOR

ABOVE CENTRAL DOOR AND DOORS AT EITHER END:

LEFT:

82 JAMES NORTHCOTE, RA (1746–1831)
The Murder of the Princes in the Tower
The future Edward V and his younger brother, the Duke of York, were murdered in the Tower in 1483, on the orders of Richard III. This, its pendant (no. 92) and no. 32 (Square Bay) are excellent examples of Northcote's approach to history painting, and of the literary/historical subjects favoured by the 3rd Earl.

OVER CENTRAL DOOR:

84 JAMES NORTHCOTE, RA (1746–1831)
Lion Hunt, 1819
This Rubensian composition derives in part from Rubens's *Lion Hunt* (Dresden Gallery).

RIGHT:

92 JAMES NORTHCOTE, RA (1746–1831)
Richard III and the Little Princes, 1799
The future Richard III (in armour) contemplates the murder of the little princes (see no. 82).

CENTRAL CORRIDOR

WITHIN ARCHWAY AT WEST END, OPPOSITE DOOR FROM RED ROOM:

427 WILLIAM BLAKE (1757–1827)
Satan Calling up his Legions (Paradise Lost)
Probably painted *c*.1805 for the 3rd Earl's wife, who was an amateur artist, as an experiment in the use of tempera on canvas. Blake described it as 'largely painted in glazes on top of gold leaf'.

454 WILLIAM BLAKE (1757–1827)
The Last Judgement
Signed and dated 1808
Commissioned by the Countess of Egremont in 1807 and inspired by Michelangelo's *Last Judgement* in the Sistine Chapel, Rome.

WEST END, WITH INSET SCULPTURAL RELIEF:

SOUTH-WEST CORNER:

91 J. M. W. TURNER, RA (1775–1851)
Jessica (Merchant of Venice, Act II, Scene V)
Illustrates the moment when Shylock instructs Jessica to 'stop...my casements' (ie close the windows). When first exhibited in 1830, it was severely criticised, and Turner's earliest biographer wrote (1862) that 'none but a great man dare have painted anything so bad'.

END WALL, WEST END:

LEFT:

21 J. M. W. TURNER, RA (1775–1851)
The Thames near Windsor, exhibited *c*.1806–7

EAST BAY:

408 WILLIAM BLAKE (1757–1827)
Characters from Spenser's 'Faerie Queene', *c*.1825
Pencil and watercolour, varnished, on muslin mounted on panel

Bought by the 3rd Earl from the artist's widow, who in 1829 instructed him as to its care: 'Mr Blake had a great dislike to his pictures falling into the hands of the picture cleaners'.

RIGHT:

8 J. M. W. TURNER, RA (1775–1851)
Tabley, Cheshire, the Seat of Sir J. F. Leicester, Bart: Calm Morning
Painted in 1808 for Sir John Leicester, who owned eleven Turners, and bought by the 3rd Earl for 165 guineas at his sale in 1827. Tabley House, Cheshire, was built by Carr of York in 1761. The subject may have suggested the 3rd Earl's commission in 1810 of *Petworth House: Dewy Morning* (no. 636; White Library).

NORTH WALL, LEFT OF CENTRAL ARCH INTO SQUARE BAY:

LOWEST REGISTER:

27* W. F. WITHERINGTON (1785–1865)
Fête in Petworth Park, 1835
The second of two great summer feasts laid on by the 3rd Earl for 6,000 local people.

The Last Judgement; by William Blake, 1808 (no. 454; North Gallery)

RIGHT OF CENTRAL ARCH:

TOP REGISTER:

402 HENRY FUSELI, RA (1741–1825)
Macbeth and the Witches (Act I, Scene III)
Painted in 1793/4 for Woodmason's abortive scheme for a rival Shakespeare Gallery to Alderman Boydell's (see no. 61; Square Dining Room). Another Shakespearean painting by Fuseli hangs opposite (no. 50).

449 WASHINGTON ALLSTON, ARA (1779–1843)
Jacob's Dream
Allston, an American painter, began this picture in 1817 and it was bought by the 3rd Earl at the Royal Academy exhibition in 1819 where it inspired Wordsworth's lines:

> But rooted here, I stand and gaze
> On those bright steps that heavenward raise
> Their practicable way.

BOTTOM REGISTER:

106 THOMAS GAINSBOROUGH, RA (1727–88)
Rocky Wooded Landscape with Rustic Lovers by a Pool
Painted *c.*1774–7, and presumably acquired by the 3rd Earl.

60 ANGELICA KAUFFMAN, RA (1741–1807)
Diomed and Cressida
A depiction of *Troilus and Cressida* (Act V, Scene II) for Boydell's Shakespeare Gallery.

END, FIREPLACE WALL:

LEFT, MIDDLE REGISTER:

5 J. M. W. TURNER, RA (1775–1851)
The Thames at Weybridge
Painted *c.*1806 and in the possession of the 3rd Earl by 1819.

ABOVE FIREPLACE:

TOP:

695 THOMAS PHILLIPS, RA (1770–1845)
The 3rd Earl of Egremont (1751–1837) in the North Gallery
This is the finest of Phillips's fifteen portraits of the 3rd Earl, which was painted shortly after his death. In the background is the North Bay with paintings by Hilton, Turner and Leslie shown hanging on the back wall. It also depicts Flaxman's *St Michael* and Carew's *Venus, Vulcan and Cupid.*

Macbeth, Banquo and the Witches (from William Shakespeare's 'Macbeth', Act I sc.iii) by Henry Fuseli, 1793/4

268 THOMAS PHILLIPS, RA (1770–1845)
The Allied Sovereigns at Petworth, 24 June, 1814
Signed and dated 1817
The 3rd Earl is shown welcoming the Prince Regent and Tsar Alexander I of Russia in the Marble Hall, while the King of Prussia, Frederick William III, faces him, and their respective suites look on. The Allied Sovereigns visited England on 6–27 June 1814, after the Peace of Paris.

4 J. M. W. TURNER, RA (1775–1851)
Windsor Castle from the Thames
Exhibited *c.*1806, demonstrating Turner's interest in classical forms of composition and debt to Gaspard Dughet, as, most obviously, in his *Narcissus and Echo* of 1804 (no. 46).

WITHIN ARCHWAY AT EAST END:

The framed embroidery in silk and metal thread on linen is English, *c.*1559–88, and is emblazoned with the sixteen quarterings of Robert Dudley, Earl of Leicester (1532/3–88), Elizabeth I's favourite.

SOUTH WALL, EAST END:

659 JOHANN ZOFFANY, RA (1733–1810)
Mrs Abington as the Widow Bellmour in Arthur Murphy's 'The Way to Keep Him'
The play was first produced at Drury Lane in 1760. The role of the widow was first played by Mrs Cibber, then by her successor, Mrs Abington.

NORTH OR SQUARE BAY

WALL OPPOSITE FIREPLACE:

CENTRE, ABOVE:

13 WILLIAM OWEN, RA (1769–1825)
Mrs Robinson
Shown hanging above the chimneypiece opposite in Turner's *c.*1827 view of the gallery, this beautiful portrait of an unknown 'Mrs Robinson' shows the competence of this forgotten artist, who was portrait painter to the Prince Regent.

CENTRE, BELOW:

33 J. M. W. TURNER, RA (1775–1851)
Ships Bearing up for Anchorage ('The Egremont Seapiece')
Possibly the first painting by Turner to enter the 3rd Earl's collection, probably at the 1802 Royal Academy exhibition and certainly by 1805. The numerous preliminary studies for this early masterpiece indicate Turner's care to depict accurately 'ships sailing, coming up into the wind, shortening sail and dropping anchor'. It is flanked by four other landscapes by Turner: (no. 46) *Narcissus and Echo* (exhibited 1804); (no. 108) *The Thames at Eton* (exhibited 1808), which is probably a pendant to (no. 653) *Cockermouth Castle* (exhibited 1810), depicting the 3rd Earl's Cumberland seat; and (no. 39) *The Forest of Bere* (exhibited 1808), which is a few miles north of Havant, Hampshire.

NORTH WALL, BOTTOM REGISTER:

LEFT:

34 CHARLES ROBERT LESLIE, RA (1794–1859)
Sancho and the Duchess
Exhibited at the Royal Academy in 1824 and illustrating a scene from Cervantes's novel *Don Quixote*.

Mrs Robinson; by William Owen (no. 13; North Gallery)

RIGHT:

31 CHARLES ROBERT LESLIE, RA (1794–1859)
Gulliver presented to the Queen of Brobdignag
A scene from Swift's *Gulliver's Travels*, painted as a companion to no. 34 and exhibited at the Royal Academy in 1835.

FIREPLACE WALL:

TOP LEFT:

30 WILLIAM HILTON, RA (1786–1839)
The Rape of Europa
Painted in 1818 for Sir John Leicester, and bought by the 3rd Earl at his sale in 1827 for 250 guineas. This was apparently Hilton's first commission, the composition being perhaps inspired by Titian's *Rape of Europa* (Isabella Stewart Gardner Museum, Boston).

ABOVE FIREPLACE:

309 Sir JOSHUA REYNOLDS, PRA (1723–92)
The Death of Cardinal Beaufort (Henry VI, Part II, Act III, Scene III)
Painted in 1789 for Boydell's Shakespeare Gallery, it depicts the death of Cardinal Henry Beaufort (1377–1447), Chancellor of England, as Lords Warwick and Salisbury (left) and Henry VI look on. Reynolds is said to have used a coal-heaver and an organ grinder as models for the Cardinal and the King. Bought in 1805 by the 3rd Earl and in a ruined state due to Reynolds's use of bitumen.

BELOW:

649 J. M. W. TURNER, RA (1775–1851)
Near the Thames Lock, Windsor
Exhibited 1809

TOP RIGHT:

24 JOHN HOPPNER, RA (c.1758–1810)
Sleeping Nymph with Cupid
Painted for Sir John Leicester in 1806 and bought at his sale in 1827 by the 3rd Earl. Hoppner is said to have considered it his masterpiece.

SCULPTURE

ARRANGEMENT

The present arrangement (devised in 1991–3) was designed to restore as far as possible that conceived by the 3rd Earl. Turner's view of the gallery shows that the two Antique Roman seated figures (nos 15, 19) were already in place in the Central Corridor on either side of the great arch. He also shows Flaxman's *St Michael overcoming Satan* (no. 97; before 1817–26) in the centre of the Square Bay, in fact just off-centre and towards the north wall, where it is located on a unique ground plan of the 3rd Earl's statue deployment drawn up in 1835 by H. W. Phillips, which has been used as the basis of the present arrangement.

Apart from the Flaxman, the Square Bay has become a gallery of works by the Irish sculptor J. E. Carew, many of which were placed here in 1835. The archway at the entrance to the Square Bay is dominated by Carew's colossal groups: (left) *Vulcan, Venus and Cupid* (no. 115; c.1827/8–31) and (right) *Prometheus and Pandora* (no. 116; 1835–7). The former is shown in this position in Phillips's full-length portrait of the 3rd Earl (no. 695; Central

Corridor overmantel), and the latter has been brought into the gallery as the only suitable pendant. Although there is further circumstantial evidence that the *Vulcan, Venus and Cupid* was originally intended for the North Gallery, it was installed in the newly constructed Audit Room (now the tea-room) by 1837, where it was balanced at the other end by Carew's *Prometheus and Pandora*.

SOUTH CORRIDOR

ANTIQUE SCULPTURE

EAST END AND LEFT SIDE:

1 *Statue of Ganymede*, Roman, second century AD; Pentelic marble. Restored, published and engraved by Bartolomeo Cavaceppi (1716–99), who provided a new head and right arm, and added the eagle's beak and the lower half of the left wing. He also reworked the surface and patinated it with chlorine to unify the original fragment and the accretions. It was imported in 1763, and has never been cleaned. Ganymede, a shepherd, was the beautiful son of Tros, the legendary King of Troy. According to Ovid, the amorous Jupiter, having transformed himself into an eagle, carried off the youth to be his cup-bearer on Olympus.

3 *Female Portrait Statue*, Roman adaptation of a Greek original of the late fifth century BC; Parian marble. Restored by Cavaceppi, who added the nose, arms and the attributes of Ceres, the goddess of agriculture (the corn, etc. in the right hand). Traditionally called 'Agrippina as Ceres', and the face indeed resembles that of Agrippina the Younger.

4 *Statue of Hera*, Roman, after a Greek or Hellenistic original, probably of the second century BC; Parian marble. Hera (Juno in Latin) was the sister and wife of Zeus (Jupiter) and was worshipped as the protectress of women. This is probably the 'Juno' imported in 1763. The head, right arm and left hand are eighteenth-century restorations.

5 *Statue of Apollo* ('Apollo Egremont'), Roman, second century AD; Parian marble. Apollo is depicted as *Apollo Kitharoedos* with his lyre (*kithara*) as patron of poetry and music and leader of the Muses. There are numerous restorations, including the nose, the right arm, the lower part of the left leg and sections of the lyre. From the Palazzo Vettori, Rome, but probably the 'Statue of Apollo' bought by Hamilton from Cavaceppi on 26 May, 1758.

6 *Statue of a Satyr Pouring out Wine*, second century AD after an original by Praxiteles; Parian marble. The torso was found near Rome in 1760 by the painter, archaeologist and dealer Gavin Hamilton (see p. 80). The head, the arms and the lower part of the right leg are the principal additions by Pietro Pacilli. The Antique support is inscribed: 'ΑΠΟΛΛΩΝΙΟΣ ... ΕΠΟΙΗΣ' ('Apollonios ... made [this]'). Hamilton assumed that the statue was by Apollonios, the first century AD Athenian sculptor who signed the Torso Belvedere in the Vatican, but the signature is of Apollonios of Aphrodisias in Caria (modern Turkey), one of a family of sculptors.

9 *Statue of an Athlete*, Roman copy of the early second century AD in Polykleitan style; Italian marble. Known as the '*Petworth Oil-Pourer*', the Antique Praxitelean head was added by the restorer. Probably the 'Statue of an Athlete' bought from the Marchese Verospi and restored by Cavaceppi.

27 *Colossal Female Head*, Greek, possibly fourth century BC; Pentelic marble. Made up from fragments of two separate colossal full-length statues into a single bust. Recent research suggests that the original fragments may have belonged to two Athenian statues of the fourth century BC. If so, this heroic bust is one of the great treasures of the Petworth collection of Antique sculpture. Possibly the 'Colossal Head' of 'Juno' bought in 1760 from the Palazzo Verospi.

NEO-CLASSICAL SCULPTURE

LEFT, EAST END:

105 J. C. F. ROSSI, RA (1762–1839)
Celadon and Amelia
Exhibited at the Royal Academy in 1821. The subject is taken from Thomson's *Seasons* and depicts the moment in *Summer* when Celadon and Amelia, the 'matchless pair' of lovers, are overtaken by a thunderstorm (Amelia is about to be struck dead by a lightning bolt). They were on the point of entering a cottage, and this may explain why this position – in front of a false door – was chosen by the 3rd Earl. The unusually dramatic conception of this group sets it apart from most contemporary British sculpture.

CENTRE:

101 JOHN FLAXMAN, RA (1755–1826)
Pastoral Apollo
Signed and dated 1825
The 3rd Earl's first commission of an ideal subject, depicting Apollo as the protector of shepherds. It took Flaxman twelve years to complete.

CENTRAL CORRIDOR

ANTIQUE SCULPTURE

WEST END, RIGHT SIDE:

Group of Pan and Olympus (Daphnis), Roman, Parian marble. Pan, the lustful Greek god of woods and fields, flocks and herds, instructs Daphnis, the blind shepherd boy, to play his invention, the syrinx (reed pipes arranged in a row of ascending length). Set within the wooden plinth is a Greek votive relief (no. 13) of the fifth century BC. Bought by the 3rd Earl for £126 at the 1801 sale of the Earl of Bessborough at Roehampton. It was restored by Pietro Pacilli (1716–72) and Vincenzo Pacetti (1746–1820), who gave Olympus (Daphnis) an Antique head, probably originally of Dionysos.

14 *Torso, restored as Dionysos*, Roman; Italian marble. This Antique torso 'from Rome, and taken out of the Tiber' was given legs and arms by J. E. Carew and the marble mason James Welch in 1832–5. Carew's new head retains evidence of patination that he employed to marry up his additions to the Antique torso, which was probably bought on the 3rd Earl's behalf by Turner in Rome in 1828.

15 *Seated Statue of a Man (Menander)*, Roman, second century AD; the head, of the Emperor Gallienus (c. AD218–68), is third century AD; Pentelic marble. Listed in the Barberini Collection, Rome, in 1738 'without a head, without one arm and lacking a foot'. These shortcomings were rectified in the mid-eighteenth century when the head (also from the Palazzo Barberini) was added. It was bought in 1760 and imported to Britain in 1763.

EAST END:

19 *Seated Statue of a Philosopher*, Attic, *c.* second century AD; Pentelic marble. Another statue from the Palazzo Barberini, Rome, where in 1738 it was described as lacking a head and an arm, but apparently sold to the 2nd Earl by Cavaceppi in 1760. The head, added by the mid-eighteenth-

The South Corridor in the North Gallery

century restorer, is Antique and reminiscent of portraits of Demosthenes, the Athenian orator. Imported in 1763.

WEST END, LEFT SIDE (IN NICHE):

11 *Statue of a Mourning Woman*, Hellenistic sepulchral statue, second or third century BC, in remarkably good, if weathered, condition. Probably bought in 1760 from the Marchese Verospi.

NEO-CLASSICAL SCULPTURE

RELIEF SET INTO WALL, WEST END:

111 Sir RICHARD WESTMACOTT, RA (1775–1856)
The Dream of Horace
Exhibited at the Royal Academy in 1823 and subsequently installed in its present position within a blocked-up window. The unusual subject was chosen by the 3rd Earl. Taken from Horace's *Ode to Calliope* (the Muse of Epic Poetry), it depicts a sleeping boy (Horace) protected by Venus, Minerva

and Apollo against wild animals. Thus protected, he need not fear the distant barbarians, even 'the cruel race of Britain'. The face of Venus (far left) was taken from 'the mistress of some man about in society', perhaps the 3rd Earl.

RIGHT:

98 Sir RICHARD WESTMACOTT, RA (1775–1856)
Nymph and Cupid
Exhibited in 1827 as 'Cupid made Prisoner', this group is typical of the mythological works produced by Westmacott during the 1820s under the influence of contemporary Italian sculpture, and of Canova in particular.

OTHER END OF CENTRAL CORRIDOR:

103 JOHN EDWARD CAREW (1785–1868)
Arethusa
The first work by Carew to be acquired by the 3rd Earl – directly from Carew's London studio in 1823. According to Ovid (*Metamorphoses*, 5, 572–641), the goddess Diana transformed the nymph Arethusa into a stream to protect her from

Bust of the 3rd Earl of Egremont (detail)

the amorous advances of a river-god. Carew depicts her with a greyhound (without classical authority) as a companion of Diana.

SQUARE BAY

NEO-CLASSICAL SCULPTURE

97 JOHN FLAXMAN, RA (1755–1826)
St Michael overcoming Satan
Signed and dated 1826
This masterpiece, which would have inspired thoughts of Milton's *Paradise Lost*, and for which the Square Bay was designed, is the 3rd Earl's supreme sculptural commission. He later recorded that he 'gave Flaxman the order and the subject, and the attitude according to the picture by Raphael'

(Louvre, Paris). Ordered before April 1817 and finished in 1826, it was carved (apart from the spear) from a single block of marble at a cost of £3,500.

JOHN EDWARD CAREW (1785–1868)
The remaining statues and busts are by this Irish sculptor and former assistant to Sir Richard Westmacott, who was showered with commissions by the 3rd Earl from 1823. The busts are (anticlockwise from right of fireplace) (no. 107) *The 3rd Earl of Egremont* (1831–4); (no. 108) *Mrs John (Harriet) King* (1831–4), the 3rd Earl's daughter; (no. 109) *General Sir Henry Wyndham* (1830–2), the 3rd Earl's second son; and (no. 110) *Lord John Townshend* (1830–2).

IN CORNERS:

115 *Venus, Vulcan and Cupid*, c.1827/8–31
Carew stated that he began work on this colossal group 'about 1827 or 1828' and that it was completed before 1831, but his assistant remembered that it was made in London and finished by 1828, so the exact dates are unclear. It was originally intended for this position, to which it was returned in 1992. Vulcan, the god of fire and the blacksmith of the gods, is seated on his anvil inscribed *AITNA* (ie Etna, the Sicilian volcano – the word 'volcano' derives from Vulcan), resting his hammer. He is accompanied by his wife Venus, and her son, Cupid, whose wings he forged.

RIGHT:

116 *Prometheus and Pandora*, c.1835–7
Carew declared in 1837 that the *Prometheus* group 'was begun about two years since' and it remained unfinished after the 3rd Earl's death in 1837. Carew claimed £4,000 'when finished' in his unsuccessful court action against Egremont's executors. In Greek mythology, Prometheus created the first man from clay, stole fire from the gods to give to mankind, was punished by Jupiter and released from his torment by Hercules. His sister-in-law was Pandora, the 'all-gifted', who was fashioned from clay by Vulcan. After Prometheus's theft of fire, Jupiter's retribution on mankind was to open Pandora's box, thus releasing all the world's evils. Only Hope remained inside.

FAR LEFT, NORTH–WEST CORNER:

102 *The Falconer*, *c*.1827/8–9

According to Carew's own testimony, it was certainly completed before his move from London to Brighton in 1831, and was installed at Petworth in 1829. Unlike Carew's other ideal statues, it apparently has no literary or mythological source; it may originally have been intended for the Duke of St Albans, who was Grand Falconer of England. In 1835 it stood at the west end of the Central Corridor, was moved into the Audit Room after *c*.1865, and returned to the North Gallery in 1992.

FAR RIGHT, NORTH–EAST CORNER:

100 *Adonis*, 1823–5/6

The 'first Commission Lord Egremont gave me', remembered Carew, as a companion to the *Arethusa* (no. 103), which the 3rd Earl bought in 1823. The *Adonis* is in fact on a larger scale and was valued by Carew at £1,500. Adonis, famous for his beauty, is depicted in the throes of his fatal struggle with a boar.

FURNITURE

The black and gold table is probably Florentine, *c*.1690. From a group of five still in the house, and described in the 1749/50 inventory, it is an important survival of the furniture acquired by the Proud Duke. It has, however, been redecorated, and its marble top has been replaced in wood, probably in the nineteenth century. Otherwise, it is a pair to the table in the Grand Staircase.

The North Bay in the North Gallery

GLOBE

ON TABLE:

The terrestrial globe by Emery Molyneux (d.1598–9) is dated 1592 and is the earliest such English globe in existence. Molyneux's terrestrial and celestial globes were hailed at the time as the 'first soe published in Christendome' intended for 'Scholars, Gentrye and Marriners'. As Petruccio Ubaldini pointed out to the Grand Duke of Tuscany in 1591, Molyneux's terrestrial globe 'distinguishes by lines of different colours and short descriptions the several voyages which Drake, Cavendish, Frobisher and others have made'. Molyneux sailed on voyages of exploration with Sir Francis Drake, and his circle included Sir Walter Ralegh. The globes were published by the London merchant-adventurer William Sanderson and dedicated to Elizabeth I, who described the terrestrial globe as the 'whole earth, a present for a prince; but with the Spanish Kings leave ...'.

The Petworth globe must have been acquired by the Wizard Earl, perhaps even from Ralegh himself, who became a close friend during their imprisonment in the Tower in the early seventeenth century. Globes are listed in both their inventories. It retains its original unvarnished surface and is in remarkably sound condition. Restoration in 1951 and 1995–7 has revealed that it is weighted with sand and made from layers of paper with a surface coat of plaster. The engraving, with elaborate cartouches, fanciful sea-monsters and other nautical decoration, is by the Fleming Jodocus Hondius (1563–1611). There are a wooden horizon circle and brass meridian ring (the hour circle and index are missing).

THE CHAPEL PASSAGE

SCULPTURE

After MICHELANGELO (1475–1564)
Pietà
This copy of Michelangelo's famous *Pietà* (1497–c.1500; St Peter's, Rome) was bought by the Proud Duke in 1691 for £108 as 'a marble statue of the old L^d. Arundell's beeing a Madonna with a dead Christ in her lap by Mich: Angelo'. It was probably carved by one of the sculptors employed by the 14th Earl of Arundel (1586–1646), such as François Dieussart (active 1622–61), but it may also be an Italian copy.

THE CHAPEL

The Chapel is the most complete interior (apart from the cellars) to survive from the medieval fortified manor house of the Percys and is still in use. It was probably constructed around the beginning of the fourteenth century. Henry, Lord Percy was given licence to crenellate in 1309, and the form of the Gothic windows and the marble colonnettes (though not the tracery or the stained glass) is most obviously in the Early English style. The wooden roof structure, consisting of 20 arch-braced trusses, originally visible but obscured by the late seventeenth-century ceiling, also survives in part. The original entrance was through a doorway with a four-centred arch at the west end of the south wall (the wall to the right of the altar). The four window openings in this wall are original, as are the blocked window embrasures on the opposite side (north wall). The Chapel originally incorporated the low and narrow corridor from which the visitor now enters, and at this end there may have been a separate chapel or chantry partitioned off from the principal space.

The medieval chapel was transformed in the late seventeenth century by the 6th Duke, who installed the plaster ceiling, the marble floor (probably) and the magnificent woodwork incorporating the family pew at the west end, and the stall and communion rail beneath. The Chapel must have been among the first ducal repairs, because by 1685 one Peter Voller was paid for the '63 Ballasters ... about inclosing Communion Table'. In 1689 Isaac Greene received £5 10s for 'ye Pulpitt in ye Chappell', and by 1691 the plasterer Edward Goudge was 'makeing ye frette worke'. Goudge, probably the most famous plasterer of his day, who worked extensively to royal commission, promised 'to doe the Chappell ceiling at Petworth ... in like manner according to the draught [drawing] made for that purpose ... for £50 noe foliage nor any other ornament to be made with any of ye pannells, excepting the two long pannells at each end'. These two decorated panels no longer survive (if they were executed at all). By 1692 George Turnour was painting and gilding the Chapel, and in the same year he and a Frenchman who supplied 'gilt sconces' received £300. Turnour's painting in imitation of walnut and his gilding still survive – a rare survival of documented seventeenth-century decoration.

The Chapel

In 1702 the Duke turned his attention to the areas on either side and above the Chapel. In the process of blocking up the windows on the north side (to the left of the altar), he ensured that the early seventeenth-century heraldic glass was recorded before being taken 'very carefully out of the windows' and 'carefully layde up'. The glass was substituted by painted heraldry (celebrating in part the Duke's own lineage) within *trompe l'oeil* windows so that the previous appearance of the Chapel was maintained. This alteration seems to have been due to the instability of the north wall. By 3 November 1702 the roof too had been repaired: 'The Healing over the Chappell is done and all the lead works relating thereto.' The Duke's attention then turned to 'the great roomes over the chapele' – the Old Library with its large window above the principal east window of the Chapel – and to the means of access to it. The Duke requested a drawing: 'so that I may make out … what sort of stayr case I can have at the end by the chaple to goe up to ye roomes over the Chaple.'

The interior of the Chapel is one of the most complete Baroque conceptions in England. Apart from the filling-in of the area beneath the balcony and the insertion of entrance steps from the raised corridor (alterations carried out by the 3rd Earl in 1793–4), the ducal fittings remain intact. The most magnificent element is the wooden painted festoon curtain above the family pew with angels supporting the ducal arms and coronet in the centre. This theatrical conceit makes the family pew tantamount to a royal box in an Italian opera house and owes much to Roman Baroque.

STAINED GLASS

The armorial stained glass was made around 1600, probably in London or Oxford, and records the various alliances of the Percy family. It has been reshuffled in the course of the 1702 and subsequent alterations. The heraldic cartouches in the east window may have originally belonged in the four south windows, reflecting the arrangement of the *trompe l'oeil* 'glass' in the blind windows on the opposite wall. The missing coat of arms of the 9th Earl of Northumberland was recreated (2000–1) for the east window (bottom right).

FURNISHINGS

The 1749/50 inventory indicates that the ducal furnishings were crimson: '10 Chairs' and various stools in the 'Gallery' (the family pew) were upholstered in velvet. Beneath, in the 'body of ye Chappel', there were '2 Stools cover'd with Crimson Velvet', while baize was considered adequate for '5 long Stools'. The gallery was also provided with a Persian carpet. The altar was covered with a 'Crimson Velvet cloth', and there were '3 damask cloaths for the Minister['s] seats' (in c.1685). Before the space was filled in in 1793–4, there were 'Two long forms under the Gallery'.

In 1817 a pedestal was made 'for the marble Madonna in the Chapel', presumably the copy of Michelangelo's *Pietà* subsequently moved to the North Gallery and now in the Chapel Passage. The cast-iron stove, to the left of the altar, is presumably the 'Arnott stove' installed in 1847–8. The bronze eagle lectern is *c.*1500, and was bought by the 8th Earl in 1582.

The painted high-back chairs, from a larger set, are probably Iberian, nineteenth-century, and may be identifiable with the '9 High back chairs' ('and 2 stools') listed here in 1869.

CHAPTER TWO

THE PARK, PLEASURE GROUND AND ESTATE

Petworth park is hallowed for its inspiration of Turner, whose landscapes, painted for the 3rd Earl in the early nineteenth century, are – with the exception of *Dewy Morning* (see illustration, p. 77) – radiant with the colours of sunset. Despite the great storms of 1987 and 1989, it is still possible to look from his landscapes through the windows of the house and identify the same scenes outside. Some 32,000 trees have been planted since then, following study of the wreckage and extensive archival research. The park beloved of Turner was the creation of 'Capability' Brown, whom the 2nd Earl of Egremont and his widow employed between 1751 and 1765 to transform the formality of the earlier layout, designed for the Proud Duke by the royal gardener George London around 1700. The history of Petworth park is, however, much more ancient, reaching back into the Middle Ages, as Horace Walpole realised when he described it as 'Percy to the backbone'.

William de Percy (1193–1245) had a 'new small park in which is his cunegaria [rabbit warren]'. In 1499 the 5th Earl of Northumberland added 105 acres, and in the course of the sixteenth century more common land was enclosed until, by 1621, the park was about 400 acres (it is now 700 acres). In 1574 the 8th Earl of Northumberland's surveyors noted two main parks ('Greate' and 'Lyttyl'), both of which were scantily planted with oak and beech. The little park, to the north-west of the house, was about 220 acres and contained '72 deare'. Its central feature, still known as Arbour Hill, had 'divers pleasant walks'. From this vantage point, it was possible to view the progress of stag-hunting in the valley beneath. Henry VIII erected a banqueting house here when Petworth became crown property on the death of the 6th Earl of Northumberland in 1537.

Petworth Park by J. M. W. Turner, c.1828–30 (no. 132; Carved Room). The park painted by Turner was created for the 2nd Earl by 'Capability' Brown in the 1750s

The Percys' fortified manor house was enclosed by walled gardens which, in 1327, contained 'certain ponds'. The bird's-eye views of Ralph Treswell (1610) and John Norden (1625) show, within new walls, the parterre and fountain installed by the 8th Earl during his extensive improvements of 1576–82. In 1610 there was a rose garden to the west, with a bowling green, orchard, fish-pond and vegetable garden beyond. The 8th Earl also laid out 'new walkes' to the north of the house, and these, also known as the birch or 'birchen' walks, were later incorporated into the Pleasure Ground. Like his father, the 9th, or 'Wizard', Earl was a keen gardener, as his library proves. Among several horticultural works was *The Gardeners Labyrinth*, an early treatise of 1579. However, despite the grandiose plans for Petworth conceived during his long imprisonment in the Tower, and the 'glorious leisure' that he enjoyed at Petworth from 1621, he seems to have left his father's arrangements largely intact, apart from constructing the huge quadrangular stables and riding school shown to the west of the house in Norden's map. By 1635 the hill running east to west from the north end of the house to the lake was terraced in ramparts or 'rampires', and this work was continued by the 10th Earl in 1636. The terraces are shown in a painting of c.1685 (illustrated on p. 59), which also depicts the extensions to the house made by the 9th and 10th Earls, the 9th Earl's stables in the foreground, and something of the gardens. They were described as 'so magnificent and complete' in 1635 by Lt Hammond, who saw 'walkes, Gardens, Orchards, Bowling Ground, Stables and Fish-Ponds' surrounding 'this Prince-like House'.

The Proud Duke wanted a grandiose setting for his new house, and George London's work for William III at Hampton Court eminently qualified him to provide it. The gardens were proceeding apace by 1689, when London was paid 'for levelling and planting the kitchen garden'. Like the 8th, 9th and 10th Earls, the Duke had a real interest in gardening, which he shared with his friend William Bentinck, 1st Earl of Portland, William III's favourite and the Superintendent of the Royal Gardens. In 1699 Portland offered to buy plants in Holland on the Duke's behalf and he would certainly have encouraged the Duke to employ London, who was both his Deputy Superintendent and Master Gardener.

A painting of c.1710 illustrated on p. 71 (Duke of Rutland collection) shows the completed west front and forecourt. To the south (on the right side of the painting) are elm walks, to the north the imposing greenhouse and to the west, 'the Vistoe from the front to Tillington', which was planted as a lime avenue, interrupted (until its demolition between 1706 and 1722) by the 9th Earl's stables quadrangle. The map of 1706 shows the layout, and the proximity of the public road to the south of the great avenue. To the north of the avenue were three terraces, 'hewn and made out of the Rocke, of 600 foote in length' (as Hammond noted in 1635), which the Duke embellished between 1689 and 1704, by realigning the steps between the terraces, and in 1692 erecting gate-piers and 'a seat that stands in the lower rampier', which were carved by John Selden. The terraces and the rest of the gardens were symmetrically ornamented with flowers in pots and clipped trees in tubs. In 1689, 'Mr Verspreetes man' (ie an employee of Antony Versprit, the foremost nurseryman of the day, and possibly the 'Dutch Gardner' mentioned in the ducal accounts) was paid 5s for 'presenting 2 potts of flowers', and a mason was paid for 'flower potts upon peeres by the Great Steppes'.

The Orangery stood at the north end of a rectangular walled orange garden, which covered an acre of ground stretching northwards from the chapel cloister at the north end of the house. This was called 'the new orange garden next ye chappell' in 1692, and within it the orange trees were set in painted 'oring tubs', which would have been placed in formal patterns within the parterres marked out by painted 'Border boards'. The Duke took a close interest in his orange trees, asking his gardener, Miller, in July 1703, 'if the orange trees are in blossom and how much' (the flowers were used to decorate the house), and on 22 August he instructed Miller to carry them back into the Orangery for over-wintering 'and not venture them abroad any longer'. At this point, the orange trees 'in double roes on each side that walk from ye house to ye oringe house' were replaced for the winter by more hardy 'Bays and Lauristinus &c. ... in two lines in the roome of the orange trees'. Thus the symmetrical effect was maintained.

This view of c.1730 attributed to Pieter Tillemans shows the huge greenhouse and terraced garden laid out to the north and west of the house by the Proud Duke (private collection)

Immediately to the west of the walled orangery garden was the flower garden, dominated by a great greenhouse to the north, between the Orangery and the terraces. In front of the greenhouse was a parterre with at least two lead statues and with a central fountain served by a fountain house on the top of the terraces. The fountain house doubled as a banqueting house and was provided with a polished marble table carved by Selden in 1696 – on 29 May 1702 the Duke's steward recorded that the Duke was 'at super in the Sumer house'. Vegetables were provided from the huge kitchen garden to the south of the house. This had been the site of the earlier kitchen garden (shown in the painting of c.1685 at Syon) and was altered and enlarged by the Duke (1689–after 1703), using bricks made in a kiln in the park. The work was supervised in its latter stages by Miller, whose son took over the general garden administration. The Duke was soon 'very much dissatisfyd with his expensive management of the kitchen garden by still keeping on winter and summer 4 men and a woman when his father never had more men formerly for the kitchen garden, rampiers &c. [ie for the whole garden].' His steward reported that the kitchen garden was 'in a

very indifferent condition' due to blight affecting the apricots, peaches, cherries, grapes, melons and currants. Nor were there any cucumbers, 'herbs, sallatting [salad] and other things for the use of the kitchen there is soe little that if your Graces ffamily were home it would not subsist them'. However, some pears, plums and 'white nutmegg peaches', 'figs and philberts' were ripe and were sent to the Duke. The Duke was unconvinced that this state of affairs was due to the weather (as the younger Miller had assured the steward), and he was sacked 'for an idle car[e]less fellow'.

Such were the Duke's domestic problems in 1703, which illustrate the small labour force in a huge formal garden, and emphasise the practical as well as aesthetic purpose of horticulture in a great establishment. Petworth was (and remains) largely self-sufficient in fruit and vegetables, and the wider estate provided venison, beef, mutton, pork and fish as well as dairy products, cereals and ice. Supplies were also sent up to London, but on 1 July 1704 the Duke was deprived of his usual baskets of plums and apricots by a nocturnal robber who 'came over the kitchen garden gates ... breaking one of the spikes on the top'.

Most of the 6th Duke's landscaping was obliterated in the return to 'nature' undertaken by 'Capability' Brown in the 1750s, and in the storm of 1987, but some of his sweet chestnuts and oaks still stand on the plateau above the former terraces. Brown's patron

The upper pond at Petworth, designed by 'Capability' Brown 1751

was the 2nd Earl of Egremont, who lost little time after inheriting Petworth in 1750 in commissioning Brown to survey the park (1751). Brown's first visit was in October 1751, when he was in his tenth year of working at Stowe in Buckinghamshire for Viscount Cobham, with whom Egremont had close family connections. Egremont was a keen landscaper and horticulturalist, and his inheritance allowed him to indulge his passion on the grandest scale and in the most fashionable style.

Brown's five contracts, worth £5,500 (beginning in 1753 and ending in 1765, two years after the 2nd Earl's death), resulted in one of his supreme creations, which was to be further developed and enriched by the 3rd Earl and his successors in the nineteenth and twentieth centuries. Today, Brown's plan remains the backbone of the Trust's management of the park, but such was the extent of the 3rd Earl's and later planting that the post-1987 storm survey concluded that none of Brown's trees had survived to be blown down by the winds.

Brown drew up his proposals for the park and Pleasure Ground on a huge map dated 1752. The

Duke's 'Iron Court' and avenue to the west were replaced by a great expanse of grass and the formal terraces on the hillside were landscaped into rolling slopes leading the eye towards the new serpentine lake in the middle distance. Ha-has to either side of the house protected the private and kitchen gardens to the south, and the Pleasure Ground to the north, from the deer, which were now able to graze right up to the west front. The margins of the park along the roadside were planted up to give the illusion that the park stretched uninterrupted for miles. The Petworth–Tillington road was moved further away from the house in 1762–4, and the fourteen-mile long park wall, already under construction by 1757, was still incomplete in 1779–80. The wider park landscape was clumped, allowing a series of irregular distant views to appear between the trees. To the north-west of the house, the 'Birchen walks', cut into straight and diagonal rides, were preserved within serpentine walks which led around the perimeter, passing the eye-catchers of the Doric summer-house and Brettingham's rotunda. Closer to the house were 'plantations of shrubs and plants of low growth that will not prevent the prospects' and 'borders adorned with flowering shrubs', many of which were bought from the Kensington nurseryman John Williamson, including arbutus, broom, honeysuckle, lilac, Persian jasmine, syringas and roses. Williamson also supplied trees for the Pleasure Ground: Scotch firs, spruce, laurels, planes, larch, limes, cedars and American maples.

About ten years after the 2nd Earl's death in 1763, his cousin, Elizabeth, Duchess of Northumberland, wrote of Brown's 'fine lawn' before the house and of the park as 'very extensive and very beautiful', containing the finest trees 'I ever saw in my life'. This implies that Brown's plantings were already looking established. They were considerably supplemented by the 3rd Earl, who inherited his father's artistic and horticultural interests, but whose prowess as an agricultural improver was unmatched by any of his line. One aspect of the continual improvements of the park and estate that tends to be overlooked was the provision of employment to the local population. The 2nd Earl's lake is said to have cost £30,000 and required

regular attention to stem the loss of water. The labour costs were such that it was said in Petworth that 'it might have been covered with copper at as little expense'. The 3rd Earl's long reign at Petworth encompassed periods of extreme hardship in the locality arising from poor harvests: in the 1790s, for example, when the price of corn was beyond the means of the poor, Egremont planted potatoes and rice to provide an alternative to bread. His enthusiasms embraced all aspects of ornamental and practical gardening and agriculture. He subscribed to gardening publications (eg *The Garden, The Botanical Magazine* and *Flora*) and, given his particular interest in arboriculture, owned and was presented with numerous books on the subject.

The 3rd Earl's improvement of the park is indivisible from his management of the agricultural estate. A member of the Board of Agriculture from 1793, he was hailed as 'one of the fathers of modern English agriculture' and was the friend of the famous agriculturalist Arthur Young, whose son, the Rev. Arthur Young, continually cites Egremont's innovations in his *General View of the Agriculture of the County of Sussex*, 1808. The Rev. Arthur Young concluded that 'his Lordship's estates are conducted upon a great scale, in the highest style of improvement'. In 1795 the *Sporting Magazine* stated that 'Everything is now conceded at Petworth to grazing and ploughing': for example, in the early 1790s the 3rd Earl began to reclaim the wooded Stag Park. Previously 'an entire forest scene', about 750 acres were 'enclosed and divided into proper fields' after the timber had been sold, 'the underwood grubbed, and burned with charcoal on the spot' and the land had been drained. Like his Wyndham and Percy predecessors, the 3rd Earl never lost an opportunity of acquiring land adjacent to his own, and the Petworth estate now increased rapidly in size, having been built up more slowly during the eighteenth century and beforehand.

The park not only contained deer, but also improved strains of cattle, sheep and even pigs. Young records that 'Lord Egremont has tried a great variety of hogs, and made many experiments'. One of these was to graze the pigs in the park during the summer: 'no corn is given: nothing but grass', after which they were slaughtered.

Turner's *Petworth Park* (no. 132; Carved Room, see illustration p. 49) includes a group of these grazing pigs in the foreground which, until recently, were assumed to be sheep. The pigs were housed in a noble piggery, an engraving of which was published by Young. This was surprisingly close to the house, and Egremont's daughter-in-law was once amazed to see 'a sow and her litter of pigs get in through a window and gallop down through the rooms'. Egremont commissioned numerous portraits of his prize cattle (painted by Boultbee and sculpted by Garrard), and his innovations included the breeding of Tibetan shawl goats, depicted in Phillips's 1798 view of the park (no. 43; Egremont collection), whose fleece was prized by London hatters. No avenue of improvement was neglected: trials were carried out (and the results published by Young) on the stocking of fish-ponds, crop rotation, the 'culture and growth' of potatoes, and the medicinal use of rhubarb and opium ('the largest quantity of this invaluable drug that was ever cured in this country, was raised in 1797 from the Earl of Egremont's garden at Petworth'); the irrigation and mulching with coal ash of parkland grass; and the use of teams of oxen, instead of horses, to draw wagons, which, despite its inefficiency, was a great enthusiasm of the 3rd Earl's. New machinery was developed such as the Suffolk plough, the Mole-Plough and 'Mr Ducket's Skim-Coulter' ('introduced by his Lordship, and with such success, that it was adopted by a number of farmers').

Lord Egremont's concern for the poor was lauded: he supplied them with a 'bounty of clothes' as well as distributing 'three and four times a week, good soup ... made of barrelled beef, Scotch barley, and potatoes, besides regaling between three and four hundred families at Christmas with beef and pork pies'. Egremont not only provided labour through the estate but was also an employer on the grandest scale by taking a lead in the local development of roads, and especially canals, which were dug by labourers drawn from amongst his own workmen. The intention was to connect London with Sussex, which was achieved largely through Egremont's investment in and chairmanship of the Wey, Rother and Arun navigations. As Young observed, this was a considerable boost to the local

economy of Surrey and Sussex, doubling the value of many estates, which were able more easily to transport 'timber, and all the production of the soil' to the London market.

Even the radical William Cobbett, who saw the park ('the very finest in the world' within a wall 'nine miles round'), acknowledged Egremont's worthiness 'of this princely estate', which the garden encyclopaedist James Loudon described in 1822 as a 'truly noble demesne'. The French-American Louis Simond was most impressed by Egremont's planting-up of the Pleasure Ground 'with the largest trees, close together, something like a heavy-timbered American forest. . . . Many of the trees were indeed American. We found here our old acquaintances the hemlock, the black spruce, the tulip-tree, the occidental plane, the acacia, and several kinds of oaks. All these trees seem to accommodate themselves extremely well with the climate of England.' Egremont had been active in planting both the park and Pleasure Ground from at least 1773, and in 1804 alone he purchased no fewer than 12,000 ash, fir, larch, birch and hornbeam. He was most interested in the acclimatisation of foreign trees and plants, about which he corresponded with Sir Joseph Banks, and Simond noted that adjacent to the North Gallery was 'the finest conservatory imaginable; the plants in the open ground and not crowded ... I never saw plants in such health and vigour; a heliotrope ten feet high, full of leaves and flowers, from the earth to the top, and perfuming the air ... No rare plants, – all for beauty and smell ... The kitchen-garden, all divided into *espalier* walls, covers thirteen acres, – not an inch of which seems unoccupied.'

The kitchen garden was indeed run on princely lines (2,550 asparagus plants were ordered in 1803), incorporating every imaginable variety of vegetables and fruit, while 'a hot house in three divisions' was erected for £400 in 1773 to grow exotics such as pineapples. The fame of the kitchen garden reached its apogee in the later nineteenth century. In 1863, according to the *Journal of Horticulture and the Cottage Gardener*, there was a staff of 20, who produced 260 melons per annum, pineapples, peaches, grapes (plants were forced to extend their season) and a huge variety of other fruits and vegetables. Although it was noted that there was a lack of flower borders at Petworth, annuals were grown to provide seed for distribution to estate workers. The 1st Lord Leconfield declared that 'a love of flowers is ever desirable from the very lowest to the very highest'. According to his daughter-in-law, Constance Leconfield, writing in 1867, the kitchen garden's 'old fashioned border' was preserved by Lady Leconfield, who wished 'not to introduce a ribbon border as was then the great fashion'. In 1878 The *Gardener's Chronicle* also focused on the kitchen garden, which now had a staff of 30, and a greenhouse was filled with pot-plants for display in the house. At about this time, the 2nd Lord Leconfield, having been told that bananas tasted better straight from the tree, sent his gardener to Kew to learn how to grow one. All the necessary paraphernalia was installed at Petworth, including a 'special green house ... which might have been the envy of Sir Joseph Paxton himself'. What followed is recounted by his grandson:

The banana tree was splendid. My grandfather took a lively interest in its progress until, lo and behold, it fructified. 'I will have that banana for dinner tonight', he said as soon as the banana was ripe. And so he did – amid a deathly hush. All were agog. The head gardener himself, controlling a great department of the estate, was not too proud to be there, concealed behind a screen between the dining-room and the serving-room. Even the groom of the chambers broke the habit of a lifetime and turned up sober to watch the event.

The banana was brought in on a lordly dish. My grandfather peeled it with a golden knife. He then cut a sliver off and, with a golden fork, put it in his mouth and carefully tasted it. Whereupon he flung dish, plate, knife, fork and banana on to the floor and shouted, 'Oh God, it tastes just like any other damn banana!' Banana tree and all were ordered to be destroyed. My famous old gardener, Mr Fred Streeter, told me that the banana cost my grandfather some £3,000.

Between the kitchen garden and the south front of the house (an area altered by Salvin in the early 1870s), there was a gigantic dragon of flowers 350 feet wide, coiled upon the grass who shed 'his skin several times during the year' and who was 'gorgeous with various kinds of bedding plants'.

After 1837 the 3rd Earl's son and grandson, the 1st and 2nd Lords Leconfield, continued to supplement the plantings in the park along traditional lines, eschewing ornamental novelties. Although there are trees surviving from the early eighteenth century, most of the trees devastated by the storms of the late 1980s had been planted since the turn of the twentieth century by the 3rd Lord Leconfield, who succeeded in 1901. Petworth House still stands at the centre of an agricultural estate, owned by Lord Egremont, whose estate yard undertakes repairs to the house and to estate buildings. Petworth is rare among country houses, whether publicly or privately owned, in retaining its traditional status within the local community, and the long family tradition of allowing free access to the park is upheld by the National Trust.

The rotunda was built for the 2nd Earl

CHAPTER THREE

PETWORTH AND THE PERCY FAMILY
(1150–1632)

The turbulent history of the Percy family is worthy of the romances of Sir Walter Scott and inspired Shakespeare. The feudal barony dates from about 1066 and from William de Percy, who came to England with William the Conqueror and died in 1096 near Jerusalem on the 1st Crusade. William de Percy's successors maintained both his close contact with the Crown and his military prowess, often with fatal results.

After 1154 William de Percy's great-grand-daughter Agnes, co-heiress to the Percy estates, married Jocelin de Louvain, who was apparently 'of handsome presence and great skill in tourney'. Before her death in 1151, Jocelin's half-sister, Queen Adeliz, widow of Henry I, gave him the Honour of Petworth. At the centre of this large estate was a fortified manor house, crenellated by royal sanction in 1309. Its proximity to the town of Petworth was typical of the time (the castle serving as a place of refuge for the inhabitants). The most evocative survival of medieval Petworth is the early fourteenth-century Chapel, whose walls and windows are adorned with the arms of the great Norman families with which the Percys allied themselves: de Gant, de Ros, de Neville, de Balliol, de Lucy. Until the late sixteenth century, however, Petworth was only an outpost of the Percys' empire. Their stronghold was in the North of England, where they owned Alnwick, Langley, Prudhoe, Newburn, Tynemouth and Warkworth in Northumberland (from which they took their principal title), Cockermouth and Egremont in Cumberland, and Topcliffe, Tadcaster, Spofforth, Leconfield and Wressell in Yorkshire. 'The North knows no prince but a Percy' was a popular saying.

Willing to risk all for power or for religion, the Percy family was a considerable political force in England throughout the Middle Ages and beyond. Richard de Percy (d.1244), a younger son of Jocelin

de Louvain and Agnes de Percy, was 'foremost among the sturdy barons who extorted the charter of English liberties from King John'. By summons to Parliament between 1298/9 and 1314, Henry de Percy (c.1273–1314) became 1st Lord Percy (by writ), acquiring Alnwick Castle, subsequently the family's chief northern seat, in 1309. Most of his life was spent fighting the Scots – he was knighted by Edward I at Berwick in 1296. His son, Henry, 2nd Lord Percy, commanded the 3rd division at Neville's Cross in 1346, where King David of Scotland was captured. His grandson (the 3rd Baron) fought in the naval action at the Sluys in 1340 and at Crécy in 1346; and his great-grandson (the 4th Baron) was present in 1356, as a boy of fourteen, at Poitiers.

In 1376 the 4th Baron, a close companion

(but later the enemy) of John of Gaunt, was made Marshal of England and in 1377 1st Earl of Northumberland. The remainder of his life was taken up with the great question of the succession to Richard II. Initially, the Percys supported Henry IV; their subsequent rebellion ended in the death at Shrewsbury in 1403 of Northumberland's son, Sir Henry Percy, immortalised as Hotspur in Shakespeare's *Henry IV*. Northumberland was pardoned, but soon allied himself with the Scots against Henry IV and was killed at Bramham Moor in 1408. His successors, as 2nd and 3rd Earls, were both embroiled in the Wars of the Roses and both died on the battlefield.

The 4th Earl regained the family's confiscated estates and served as Lord Great Chamberlain of England to Richard III, whom he deserted on the battlefield at Bosworth in 1485. Having switched his allegiance to Henry VII, he became the Tudor King's main representative in the North. For his betrayal of Richard III he was hated there and was killed at Topcliffe by a mob protesting about high taxes in 1489. The 4th Earl was a patron of John Skelton, the poet laureate, who lamented his demise in verse:

What man remembryng howe shamfully he was slaine
From bitter weping himself can constrain?

He was succeeded by his twelve-year-old son, Henry, 5th Earl, the splendour of whose establishment is commemorated in 'The Book of all the Directions and Orders for Keeping of my Lord's Household Yearly', which was published in 1770 as the *Northumberland Household Book*. The 5th Earl's household was modelled on that of the court, each grade, rank and function of his servants being described with military precision. This close attendance to domestic economy is indicative of an increasingly civilised and luxurious aristocratic way of life following the accession of Henry VIII in 1509. The 5th Earl was known as 'the magnificent'.

(Left) The seal of Henry de Percy, who became 1st Lord Percy by summons to Parliament, 1298/9–1314

(Right) Thomas Percy, 7th Earl of Northumberland; painted in 1566 (no. 501). He was executed in 1572 for supporting Mary, Queen of Scots

He was 'more like a prynce than a subject', the magnificence of his apparel and of his retinue (which included his own heralds) being notable from his earliest youth. Like Henry VIII, he wrote poetry and was exceptional for his learning.

The timetable of his day was similar to that of his Norman ancestors: mass was heard at six o'clock (a choir was on the payroll), breakfast at seven, dinner at ten and supper at four. At Leconfield, the castle gates were closed at nine, and here, the sparsely furnished principal rooms were inscribed with verse by the Earl's poets, Skelton and Lydgate. In medieval fashion, hangings and portable furniture were carried between his castles. At the Field of the Cloth of Gold in 1520, when Henry VIII met François I, Northumberland's retinue included 'twenty horses all caparisoned in trappings, of velvet embroidered in gold and silver'. In 1526 Henry VIII visited Petworth where he had 'good game and recreation'.

Northumberland's extravagance debilitated the estates. From a total annual income of £2,300, his domestic expenditure was approximately £1,500. In 1516 he fell foul of Thomas Wolsey, then Archbishop of York, and was fined £10,000. Wolsey's persecution of the old nobility was one of the factors that caused Northumberland's gradual withdrawal from military and state affairs. His son, the 6th Earl, whom he had reproved as 'a proud, licentious and unthrifty waster', and who succeeded in 1527, not only inherited his father's debts but compounded them by bad management. He had the misfortune to fall in love with Anne Boleyn, which complicated his relations with Cardinal Wolsey and the King. Condemned to a loveless and unlucrative marriage, he was dogged by illness. His brother and heir, Thomas Percy, was executed and attainted following his part in the northern Catholic rising known as the Pilgrimage of Grace in 1537; later that year, the 6th Earl himself died, having bequeathed his estates to Henry VIII.

It was not until 1557 that the 7th Earl succeeded to the title, due to his father Thomas's attainder. Although his Catholicism debarred him from office under Elizabeth I, in 1563 he entertained the Queen at Petworth, where he was encouraged to live because of suspicions about his loyalty. Indeed he viewed Mary, Queen of Scots as Elizabeth's rightful heir and fomented rebellion in the North following her imprisonment. In 1569 Northumberland and the other rebels fled to Scotland, where they were imprisoned. Three years later, he was handed over to the English government, was beheaded at York in 1572, and was beatified soon afterwards. His brother, Henry, 8th Earl, was imprisoned in the Tower on suspicion of conspiracy, and on his release, was compelled by Elizabeth I to live at Petworth from 1573 to 1576. She was keen to prolong his late brother's attainder so that the Crown could benefit from the Percy estate revenues, but even after 1576 the Earl was forbidden to travel north, despite the Queen's favour of a royal visit to Petworth in 1583. The 8th Earl now seems to have reverted to Catholicism and was gradually drawn into the Catholic plots on behalf of Mary, Queen of Scots. Imprisoned for suspected treason in the Tower in 1584, he was found shot dead eighteen months later. The official cause of death was suicide (he may have wished to spare his family yet another attainder), but he was probably murdered.

Because the 8th Earl was forced to spend more time at Petworth than any of his ancestors, he made many improvements to the house. In 1574 the Earl's officers surveyed the buildings, finding the main house essentially in good repair, 'inclosed with old walls of stone' and battlemented with brick, but the outbuildings were 'very much decayed'. Although

no plans or elevations were made, the 1574 survey reveals that Petworth was comparatively small, and could not have accommodated the full Percy household in its heyday (the 5th Earl had more than 160 servants in 1512). The 8th Earl repaired the existing buildings, built new lodgings, renovated the Chapel and created a new garden with walls and fountain at a total cost of approximately £4,500. Its general appearance, with additions made by the 9th Earl, is shown in drawings of 1610 and 1625.

Despite his own secret Catholicism, the 8th Earl brought up his eldest son, Henry, 9th Earl (1564–1632), as a Protestant and determined for his children 'wholly to bring them up in learning'. After private tuition at Petworth, the 9th Earl was sent on a tour of France, northern Italy and the Low Countries, finally settling in Paris whence he returned to England in 1582. Initially, the 9th Earl indulged (as he put it) in 'hawks, hounds, horses, dice, cards, apparel, mistresses', spending lavishly and being duped, as he later discovered, by his agents. In 1586 a 'check-roll' listed 58 members of his household, fewer than that of his predecessors, and far short of the 100 officers and servants recommended by a contemporary theorist for the entourage of an earl. At first, having inherited his father's servants, he recruited new ones 'young, handsome, brave, swaggering, debauched, wild, abetting all my young desires' and in a few years he reckoned that he had lost £60,–70,000 through extravagance and 'unadvisedly, in sales of woods, in demises of lands or sale'. Eventually he checked this headlong career into debt: 'I must confess I was forced to discard to the very kitchen boys before things could be settled as I wished.'

The 9th Earl's *Advice to his Son* is a fascinating insight into the running of a great establishment, and the 9th Earl's voluminous accounts chart the intricacies of income and expenditure within the equivalent of a huge business. In such a household, with landowning responsibilities in many counties, 'men are gathered together from all the corners of the world'. Many of the 9th Earl's principal officers were drawn from old county families with a long tradition of service to the Percys, and this loyalty extended to the lower servants. According to the 9th Earl, the first principle of efficiency was 'to understand your own estate better than any of your officers'. By taking the trouble to do this, and by buying land around Petworth and elsewhere, he had increased his annual income from £3,000 to £6,650 by 1598. By the 1620s, the net income had risen to £11,000, reaching nearly £13,000 by his death in 1632.

(Right) This bird's-eye view of the 1680s shows the immense stables in the foreground ('the finest of their Kind in all the South of England', according to Defoe), with Petworth House beyond, as it was before the Proud Duke's alterations (private collection)

(Left) A map of 1610 shows the Percys' Petworth, with the main part of the town lying to the south and east of the house and the church to the east, as they still do

The 9th Earl was 'naturally a kind of inward and reserved man', being afflicted with deafness. After his debauched and spendthrift early twenties, and military service in the Low Countries, he embraced knowledge, 'this infinite worthy mistress'. He had ample opportunity to pursue his studies when, in 1605 he was sentenced to life imprisonment for alleged complicity in the Gunpowder Plot: his distant cousin and employee, Sir Thomas Percy, who was one of the conspirators, had visited him the day the plot was revealed. He denied the charges – 'the world knows that I am no Papist' – but was fined £30,000 (he actually paid £11,000 in 1613) and imprisoned in the Tower of London until 1621. Although he had lost his freedom, there were compensations. He was lodged in luxurious and spacious apartments within the Martin Tower at the north-east corner of the fortress. His fellow prisoner was Sir Walter Ralegh, who wrote his *History of the World* (1614) during his incarceration and who is said to have presented Northumberland with the earliest surviving English globe, made by Emery Molyneux in 1592 (North Gallery). He certainly encouraged the 9th Earl's addiction to tobacco.

Northumberland had three principal scholars – the so-called 'Three Magi' – in his service: Thomas Harriott (1560–1621), American traveller, correspondent of Kepler on optics, mathematician and astronomer; Walter Warner (1550–1636), an expert on algebra who looked after the Earl's library; and Robert Hues (1553–1632), a scientific geographer who had undertaken a world voyage in 1586–8. 'Their prison was an academy where their thoughts were elevated above the common cares of life', wrote a contemporary. The 9th Earl's reputation as a scientist, astrologer and alchemist earned him the sobriquet the 'Wizard Earl', but he was noted for other branches of knowledge, as the list of books dedicated to him reveals. These not only include works of arcane philosophical speculation, but also on such subjects as the breeding of horses (he encouraged the birth of horse-racing in the 1580s and built a great equestrian establishment at Petworth in the 1620s) and the building of forts (he had served as a volunteer in the Netherlands and wrote a lengthy unpublished manuscript on the art of war).

The main source of information about the 9th Earl's interests is his library. Of the 826 printed books known to have been in his possession, 552 survive at Petworth (Egremont collection) and Alnwick; he probably owned 1,250 volumes in all, a huge number at the time. They were usually bound in vellum, with silk ties, and stamped in gold with the Percy crescent within the motto of the Order of the Garter (which Northumberland received in 1593). They include volumes on mathematics, science, medicine, geography, history, military strategy, alchemy, sorcery, gardening and architecture, many closely annotated with his observations. Works in Latin, French and Italian abound, encompassing literary classics as well as non-fiction. A group of 147 English plays includes early editions of works by the 9th Earl's contemporaries such as Shakespeare, Jonson, Webster and Marlowe. Although the books are now on open shelves in the White and Old Libraries, they were originally kept in chests within the 9th Earl's library at Petworth, according to the inventory taken on his death.

While a prisoner, the 9th Earl contemplated a grandiose rebuilding of Petworth, to which he was confined after his release in 1621. 'The Computation of the New House at Petworth' (1615) reveals that this would have cost £25,000, a vast but not impossible sum for a man receiving around £11,000 rental income a year. A ground plan, also of 1615, shows that the new house was to be built around courtyards, with a gallery of 315 feet running the full length of one of the ranges. In the event, he contented himself with merely extending the 8th Earl's house, but he did complete a huge stable courtyard, between the present house and the lake. The 'pepper pot' lodges that he built at Syon in the early 1600s were to be repeated at Petworth (but were never built), and their Neo-classical style indicates the influence of Italian and French architecture, as well as its English interpretation by Inigo Jones. (His architectural library included works by Vitruvius, Alberti, Serlio, Jacques Androuet du Cerceau the Elder, Scamozzi and Andrea Palladio.)

When the 9th Earl's son came to commission a posthumous portrait of his father from Van Dyck, it was entirely fitting that it depicted him in academical robes and in a melancholic pose indicative of his love of study and the acquisition of wisdom.

The Wizard Earl: Henry Percy, 9th Earl of Northumberland; a posthumous portrait commissioned by his son from Van Dyck (no. 223; Square Dining Room)

CHAPTER FOUR

THE 10TH EARL OF NORTHUMBERLAND

Algernon Percy, 10th Earl of Northumberland (1602–68) lived from the age of six with his tutor in the Tower of London 'to ween him from his nursery company and his mother's wings' until he went up to Cambridge in 1615. Between 1619 and 1624 he travelled widely in Holland, France and Italy in order, as his father put it, 'to gayne the tonges'. He shared the artistic interests of Charles I's court but prized the liberties of Parliament above royal absolutism. His relationship with Charles was complex. As a great nobleman of almost feudal stature and as a generous patron of Van Dyck, Northumberland had much in common with the King. As Admiral of the Fleet (1636–8), Lord

Tobias and the Angel; by Elsheimer (nos. 272–9; Somerset Room). Acquired by the 10th Earl in 1645 from the Duke of Buckingham's famous collection

High Admiral (1638–42), Commander of the Army in the second Scottish war (1639–40), and as a member of the Council, he was prominent in the King's government, while deploring the general unrest and bankruptcy caused by Charles's policies. Northumberland's eventual defection from the King's cause in 1642 was deeply felt by Charles, who complained that he had raised Northumberland to office after office and had 'courted him as his mistress, and conversed with him as his friend, without the least intermission of all possible favour and kindness'. Northumberland was critical of Charles's attempt to make Parliament an instrument 'to execute the commands of the King'.

During the Civil War, as a moderate Parliamentarian, he pursued a pacific line that earned both the respect and the suspicion of both sides. He conducted Parliament's negotiations with the King, first at Oxford in 1642/3, at Uxbridge in 1645, and after the King's defeat, at Newport in 1648. He believed that the concessions made by Charles on the latter occasion were sufficient, and wished to impose the same conditions on Charles II in 1660. He opposed both the King's execution and the prosecution of the regicides. He took no further part in public life during the Commonwealth, and although he was given honorary court posts under Charles II, by then he felt himself 'too olde for the Gallantries of a young Court'. Northumberland was termed 'the proudest man alive' by Clarendon and 'was in all his deportment a very great man'. Clarendon continued: 'Though his notions were not large or deep, yet his temper and his reservedness in discourse, and his unrashness in speaking, got him the reputation of an able and wise man.'

Algernon Percy, 10th Earl of Northumberland, his first wife, Anne Cecil, and their daughter, Katherine; by Sir Anthony van Dyck (no. 289.)

Despite his official responsibilities, his shortage of money (the Civil War is said to have cost him £42,000) and bouts of illness, Northumberland was active as a collector, patron and builder from the 1630s. As a Parliamentarian, however indigent, he was well placed to acquire pictures from royalist collections during the Civil War and the Commonwealth. In the 1630s he rented Dorset House in Fleet Street, and by 1640 was the tenant of the much grander York House, the palace of George Villiers, 1st Duke of Buckingham, whose great collection was still *in situ* in the custody of his widow and of the youthful 2nd Duke. In 1642 Northumberland's second marriage to Lady Elizabeth Howard, daughter of the 2nd Earl of Suffolk, allowed him to acquire Suffolk House,

next door to York House, at Charing Cross. While modernising his new acquisition, Northumberland continued to live at York House (until 1647), revelling in the grandeur of Buckingham's pictures and sculpture, which included paintings by High Renaissance Italian artists, by Rubens and Van Dyck as well as classical statuary (purchased from Rubens) and Bernini's *Samson Slaying the Philistine* (given by Charles I) as the centrepiece of the garden (now Victoria and Albert Museum).

In 1645, at the height of the Civil War, Parliament voted to confiscate the Buckingham collection as the property of the royalist 2nd Duke and recommended that 'superstitious' (ie Papist) pictures should be burned. When it became clear that this would result in the loss of most of the £20,000 value of the collection, Northumberland not only succeeded in preventing the destruction, but managed to acquire several highly important pictures himself as compensation for losses suffered during the Civil War. As well as a Titian double-portrait now at Alnwick, the paintings included several still at Petworth: the eight little Elsheimers (nos. 272–9; Somerset Room) and two pictures attributed to Andrea del Sarto (Egremont collection).

As a member of the 'Whitehall group' of connoisseurs, collectors and advisers that clustered about Charles I, Northumberland's tastes combined architecture, the patronage of Van Dyck and the acquisition of Old Masters and Antique statuary. With the exception of the King and the 4th Lord Wharton, no other contemporary patron owned more pictures by Van Dyck, who had become Charles I's court painter in 1632, and whose expertise and profound knowledge of the arts was a considerable inspiration to Northumberland in the development of his own aesthetic interests. The 1671 inventories of Northumberland House (previously Suffolk House) and Petworth list eighteen original Van Dycks and four copies. There are twenty Van

Dycks at Petworth today, most of which were commissioned or acquired by Northumberland. He paid Van Dyck £200 for 'Pictures of his Lo͏ᵖ. and Countesse and divers others' in 1635–6. This must refer to the portrait of the Earl, his first wife, Anne Cecil, and their daughter, Katherine (no. 289), which, like the other double portrait of Lords Newport and Goring (no. 300; Square Dining Room), was valued at £60 in 1671. The 1671 inventories reveal that the average valuation of the three-quarter-length portraits was £30. Doctrinaire Puritans would have been shocked to know that he commissioned from Van Dyck a now lost 'Crucifixion with five angels collecting the blood in five golden dishes, and beneath the Cross, the Virgin, St John and the Magdalen'.

At Petworth today is a series of three-quarter-length female portraits by Van Dyck, which were almost all in London in 1671, of Northumberland's relations, friends and connections. Although the paintings were acquired over a long period (partly by gift or bequest from the sitters, but also evidently

The Younger Children of Charles I; by Sir Peter Lely (no. 149; Somerset Room). Probably painted at Syon in 1647, when the royal children were in Northumberland's custody

by purchase), they represent a conscious emulation of the sets of portraits of famous or beautiful women that were formed on the Continent from the fifteenth century onwards. They may also have inspired the similar group of Van Dyck portraits put together by Lord Wharton at Upper Winchendon House, Buckinghamshire. Their successors include the 6th Duke of Somerset's commission to Michael Dahl and Sir Godfrey Kneller of portraits of the ladies of Queen Anne's court (in the Beauty Room).

Northumberland subsequently commissioned similar portraits from Sir Peter Lely, who was able to study the Van Dycks at Northumberland House, and whose portrait of the 10th Earl's daughter, Lady Elizabeth Percy (1648–9, no. 524; Square Dining Room) is closely based on Van Dyck's depiction of the Countess of Sunderland (no. 305; White and Gold Room, Egremont collection). In 1647 Northumberland commissioned Lely's great portrait of *The Younger Children of Charles I* (no. 149; Somerset Room), which was probably painted at Syon, when the royal children were in Northumberland's custody. Lely's employment by the Percy family continued after the 10th Earl's death (thirteen portraits by him were listed in the 1671 inventory).

As well as transforming the English tradition of portraiture, Van Dyck was influential as a collector and connoisseur, having formed a superb collection of paintings by Titian. In the confusion that followed Van Dyck's early death in 1641, Northumberland was at pains to keep track of the painter's collection. In 1646 he paid £200 for two of Van Dyck's most important paintings by Titian: the *Vendramin Family* (National Gallery) and the *Perseus and Andromeda* (Wallace Collection). In the 1671 inventory of Northumberland House, the *Vendramin Family* alone was valued at £1,000, almost a quarter of the value of the whole of Northumberland's collection, the *Perseus and Andromeda* having been sold shortly after its purchase. Northumberland had also acquired Van Dyck's unfinished equestrian portrait of Charles I, which had been left in the artist's studio at his death (no. 124; Carved Room). Another Titian listed in 1671, which may have been acquired by Northumberland on Van Dyck's advice, is the '*Naked Venus and a Satyr*' (no. 154; Somerset Room), a painting

Man in a Black Plumed Hat; by Titian, c.1515–20 (no. 298.)

of dubious quality, which was partially repainted between 1652 and 1671 following extensive damage. Titian's damaged, but undoubtedly genuine, *Man in a Plumed Hat* (no. 298), may also be listed in the 1671 Petworth inventory as one of 'Two men's pictures done to the wast, one by Jorjone [ie Giorgione], the other by Titian'.

According to the 1671 inventories of the 10th Earl's principal southern seats – Northumberland House, Petworth and Syon – the majority of the best and most valuable of his 167 paintings were, not surprisingly, kept in London, at a time when it was *de rigueur* to display one's principal works of art in the capital. At Northumberland House there were probably (ie allowing for several imprecise descriptions) about 20 Italian, 9 German, 35 Flemish, 6 English, 3 Spanish, 1 Dutch and 4 anonymous pictures (ie 80 in total valued at £3,282). At Petworth, there were 66 pictures, again with the emphasis on the Italian and Flemish schools, valued at £869. At Syon, there were only 21 pictures listed, mostly Dutch landscapes with a few, apparently Italian, paintings.

The lists and appraisal of the pictures in the Earl's houses were undertaken by Symon Stone, a painter of portraits, flower-pieces and copies, who acted as the curator of the collection from the 1640s until 1671. Connoisseurship was reasonably sophisticated in the circle of Charles I, so it is not surprising that Stone makes a clear distinction in the inventories between originals and copies, and sometimes expresses his uncertainty about an attribution. Stone's duties included helping 'to clense and ayre the pictures, keeping cleane the picture roome all the yeare' and he was paid 'for charcoles for ayring the roome'. He received £8 4s 'for keeping the pictures at Northumberland House a yeare' and was paid extra for crating pictures for transport (by boat to Syon), providing picture frames, undertaking restoration and painting copies of portraits and Old Masters for presentation to the Earl's friends. He also acted as a *cicerone*, and the fact that he was paid in 1666 for 'taking downe' and 'hanging up' pictures suggests that he was responsible for their display. In effect, he fulfilled the same role as David Teniers for Archduke Leopold Wilhelm, who bought several of Charles I's pictures in the Commonwealth sales and whose Brussels picture gallery Teniers depicted in a series of pictures, one of which is at Petworth (1651; no. 76; North Gallery).

The little we know of how the collection was displayed has to be extrapolated from Northumberland's personal papers. Stone was expressly charged with 'a picture roome', presumably at Northumberland House, and in 1637 Van Dyck's portrait of Strafford (1636; no. 311; Square Dining Room) was hanging 'in one of the Galleries' at Syon. In 1657 payments for '11 ounces of greene silke string to hang up pictures' and '10 ounces red for lookeing glasses' imply that at least some of the pictures were hung on green and (probably) red backgrounds, both standard colours as a foil for paintings and known to have been used for this purpose at York House. It is likely that the majority of Northumberland's pictures were deployed in galleries and rooms of state, with the smaller pictures perhaps gathered together in cabinet rooms or closets, just as they were in the contemporary Green Closet, which still exists at Ham House, Richmond. The accounts show that the pictures were framed in ebony or giltwood, a preponderance of ebony frames for both Northern and Italian pictures being typical of the time. Gerard Seghers's *St Sebastian* (no. 601; Little Dining Room), listed at Northumberland House in 1671, retains an ebonised and silvered carved frame which may date from the 10th Earl's lifetime, and several of the Petworth Van Dycks have seventeenth-century gilt livery frames which may also date from the 1660s.

Rare depictions of the roughly contemporary picture and sculpture galleries at Arundel House, The Strand, furnished with Italianate *sgabello* chairs of the same type that survive at Petworth, appear in Mytens's portraits of the Earl and Countess of Arundel (*c*.1618; Arundel Castle). Similar rooms, with classical detailing in the Italianate style of Inigo Jones, may well have been constructed by the 10th Earl during his alterations to Northumberland House in 1642–9 and 1655–7. His architect was Edward Carter, Jones's successor as Surveyor of the King's Works, through whom several royal craftsmen were employed. As at Arundel House, the gardens overlooking the river at

Two of the 9th or 10th Earl's Italianate chairs (Staircase Hall)

Northumberland House were peopled with statues. In 1645–7, Northumberland had acquired bronze statuary from Windsor Castle but this was displaced in 1657–8, when marble statues were raised on six painted wooden plinths in the 'Tarries [ie terrace] walke'. These and other Antique marble busts and statues had been in Charles I's collection and were returned to the Crown by Northumberland in 1660. It is possible, however, that the Petworth collection may still contain Antique statuary acquired by the 10th Earl.

The 10th Earl also made extensive alterations to the gardens at Syon, where he employed a 'French gardener', possibly André Mollet, in 1639–40. His principal alterations to Petworth, conducted in the 1630s, also related to both the house and its surroundings. At all three of his principal southern seats, the 10th Earl was concerned over a period of more than 30 years with the *tout ensemble* as a setting for his collections. At Petworth, between 1632 and 1634, the 10th Earl spent at least £4,500 on repairs and building work as well as on furnishings that included tapestries worth more than £1,000, four beds 'with chayres, stooles and ffurniture suitable', and 'carpettes of turkey worke'. Most of these furnishings no longer survive, but in 1635–6 he purchased 'backstooles of the Italian fashion', which are probably the black and gold *sgabello* hall-chairs bearing the Percy crescent that still stand beneath the Grand Staircase.

The 10th Earl's architectural patronage was considerable and was largely extended to royal architects and craftsmen, but little remains as visible evidence of his discrimination, as Northumberland House, Syon and Petworth were all transformed in the late seventeenth and eighteenth centuries. His interests embraced all the arts. He bought 'cheny plate' (ie Chinese porcelain) in 1644–5, and one of the greatest Dutch silversmiths, Christian van Vianen, supplied him with crested silver plate in c.1636–42 (a salver and covered bowl survive in the Duke of Northumberland's collection). His interest in contemporary fashion continued throughout his life.

The 10th Earl had followed his own father's example in taking particular trouble over the education of his heir, Joceline, Lord Percy, born in 1644 at York House. John Evelyn thought that, as a

Joceline Percy, 11th Earl of Northumberland; attributed to Sir Peter Lely (no. 536.)

result, the 10th Earl had given *'a citizen to his country'*. 'It is not enough', wrote Evelyn in 1658 after Lord Percy's return from Italy, 'that persons of my Lord Percy's quality be taught to dance and to ride, to speak languages and weare his cloathes with a good grace (which are the verie shells of travail); but besides all these that he know men, customs, courts and disciplines, and whatsoever superior excellencies the places afford, befitting a person of birth and noble impressions.' In 1670, two years after the death of his father, the 11th Earl set out again for Italy with his pregnant Countess and their daughter. They were accompanied by the philosopher John Locke, who was travelling as their physician. Lady Northumberland was detained by illness in Paris, while her husband pressed on to Turin. Here he died on 21 May 1670, having 'heated himself by travelling post for many days'. A few weeks later, his widow gave birth to a still-born child (an infant son had died in 1669). The earldom of Northumberland and the other Percy honours were now extinct, but the 11th Earl's three-year-old daughter, Elizabeth, inherited his ancestral estates.

CHAPTER FIVE

THE PROUD DUKE

The Percy inheritance brought Lady Elizabeth many years of misery. Her widowed mother having married Ralph Montagu (later 1st Duke of Montagu) in 1673, she became the ward of her grandmother, the widowed second wife of the 10th Earl. The Dowager Lady Northumberland was 'a divell of a woman', whose grand plans for her ward embroiled them both in a series of disgraceful incidents. In 1679, when Lady Elizabeth was twelve, she was married to the seventeen-year-old Henry Cavendish, Earl of Ogle. Lord Ogle has usually received a bad press. He was certainly described by one of his young bride's relations as 'the sadest creature of all kindes that could have bine founde fit to be named for my Lady Percy, as ugly as anything young can be'. However, he was also said to have 'a quick and ready understanding' and to be 'a marvellous brisk forwardly young man'. He died the following year on a continental tour, his wife having returned to the schoolroom.

Such was the glamour of the young widow (she had everything except good looks) that Charles II repeated his attempt of February 1679 to interest the Dowager Lady Northumberland in a match with his third son by the Duchess of Cleveland. This would have brought back the Northumberland title into the family, as the young man had been created Earl of Northumberland in 1674. However, the King was unable to raise enough money to satisfy Lady Elizabeth's grandmother, who also had no wish to marry her ward to a bastard, even a royal one. Instead, she was given to an unsavoury rake, Thomas Thynne of Longleat, Wiltshire, nicknamed 'Tom o' ten thousand' because of his great wealth. Having bribed Lady Northumberland, Thynne engineered the match against the wishes of Lady Elizabeth, who found him so repulsive that she soon fled to Holland. Before being forced into this unwelcome marriage, Lady Elizabeth had fallen in love with Count Karl von Königsmark, a colourful adventurer, with whom she took up again after her escape to the Continent. Königsmark, a mercenary by profession, then instigated the murder of Thynne, who was returning home from an evening with his crony, the Duke of Monmouth. Königsmark was acquitted, perhaps by the intervention of Charles II, but his three paid assassins were hanged.

The Proud Duke: Charles Seymour, 6th Duke of Somerset; by John Closterman, 1692 (no. 129; Carved Room)

In 1682 the twice-widowed Lady Elizabeth at last formed a more suitable and lasting alliance with the 6th Duke of Somerset. Her former exploits (and her red hair) were lampooned by Swift in 1711:

Beware of *Carrots* from Northumberland
Carrots sown *Thyn* a deep root may get,
If so they are in *Sommer set*
Their *Conyngs mark* them, for I have been told
They assassine when young and poison when old.

Charles Seymour, 6th Duke of Somerset (1662–1748), known as the 'Proud Duke', has become something of a caricature due to the stories about his inordinate pride and pomposity. He corrected his second Duchess, Lady Charlotte Finch (his first wife having died in 1722), for over-familiarity (she had tapped him with her fan): 'Madam, my first Duchess was a Percy, and *she* never took such a liberty.' Lady Charlotte was chosen sight unseen on the basis of coded reports by his chaplain, which described her as if she was a book. The Duke forgot his own code and had to get more explicit guidance from 'Beau' Nash. One of his daughters had the temerity to sit down in his presence (he had fallen asleep) and had £20,000 docked from her inheritance. A servant was dismissed for turning his back on the Duke while using a bellows at the fire (a difficult operation to manage facing forwards). When travelling, the ways were cleared before the ducal carriage so that he would not be exposed to the gaze of the vulgar. On one occasion a swineherd refused to be moved away: 'I shall see him and my pig will see him too', he declared. In 1702, the then 42-year-old Duke was described as 'of middle stature, well shaped, a very black complexion, a lover of musick and poetry; of good judgement but by reasons of great hesitation in his speech, wants expression'. According to the prejudiced Swift, of judgement he had 'not a grain, hardly common sense' and he was also said to have 'always acted more by humour than reason'. Swift mentions his 'imperious manner' and he was 'humoursome, proud and capricious', according to another source. To Macaulay, he was a 'man in whom the pride of birth and rank amounted almost to a disease'.

Elizabeth Percy, Duchess of Somerset, with her son, Algernon; by John Closterman (no. 127; Carved Room)

The Proud Duke was none the less an energetic builder, patron, collector and benefactor as well as a prominent courtier and soldier. Perhaps he revelled in his ducal rank and royal lineage because his succession to the dukedom of Somerset was somewhat fortuitous. Until the premature death of the 3rd Duke in 1671, he had 'no more prospect of a dukedom than of the Crown itself'. His brother became the 5th Duke at the age of seventeen, on the death of a cousin in 1675, but was murdered in Italy by a jealous husband three years later. At this time, he was only sixteen and probably at Trinity College, Cambridge, to which he was later to become a considerable donor. Despite his brother's unfortunate demise, the new Duke followed in his footsteps, and made a Grand Tour between 1679 and 1681. His marriage in 1682 to Lady Elizabeth

Percy, the greatest heiress of the day, thus added to his high position the only element previously wanting: a large fortune.

One of the conditions of his marriage was that he should change his surname from Seymour to Percy in honour of his wife's huge inheritance. To his evident relief, his wife absolved him of this requirement when she came of age in 1687/8. Her majority was more significant in that it gave the Duke full control of his wife's riches, thus allowing him to put in train (among other grand schemes) the transformation of Petworth into a ducal seat. That Petworth was rebuilt in the style most closely associated with Louis XIV is indicative of the Duke's absolutist tendencies, but also reveals the influence of his Francophile stepfather-in-law, Ralph Montagu, four times Ambassador to the French Court between 1666 and 1678, whose London house in Bloomsbury (on the site of the British Museum) and whose country seat at Boughton, Northamptonshire, bear close similarities to Petworth. Montagu's French connections, Louis XIV's expulsion of the Huguenots in 1685, and William III's accession to the English throne in 1688 were three significant factors that brought French and Dutch designers and craftsmen into England and encouraged the spread of the Franco-Dutch Baroque style. Given the 6th Duke of Somerset's elevated position at Court and Montagu's prolonged Mastership of the Great Wardrobe (from 1671), which controlled the furnishing of the royal palaces, he was well placed to employ royal craftsmen for the rebuilding and refurnishing of Petworth.

Both Montagu (probably) and William III (certainly) employed the Huguenot Daniel Marot, William's *dessinateur en chef*, whose style was widely disseminated throughout northern Europe by means of engravings (for example of his interiors at Het Loo, William III's principal Dutch palace). Marot, who had previously worked for Louis XIV's *maître ornemaniste* (master designer) Jean Berain, is likely to have accompanied William III to England soon

The unusual pediments on the west front are very similar to this chimneypiece design (c.1697–1700) for De Voorst by Daniel Marot

after his and Queen Mary's acceptance of the crown in February 1689. This would have allowed him to design the west front of Petworth (not completed until 1702) as well as the Marble Hall (largely finished in 1692). Elements of both are strongly comparable to Marot's work elsewhere, and the truncated central dome of the west front (destroyed in 1714; rebuilt soon afterwards and subsequently removed in 1777–8) was also a feature of the façade of Montagu House, Bloomsbury (1686–8), and of the stable block at Boughton. The west front is also similar to Marot's De Voorst, near Zutphen, built c.1695 for William III's favourite, the Earl of Albemarle, a friend and correspondent of the

The west front of Petworth as rebuilt by the Proud Duke; from a painting of c.1710 in the collection of the Duke of Rutland

Proud Duke. The Duke paid 'Mr Maro' £20 in 1693, and 'Monsr. Marot' is also known to have borrowed a book from the ducal library. However, the attribution to Marot is slightly obscured by James Dallaway's assertion (*History of West Sussex*, 1832) that the architect of Petworth was 'Pouget, a Frenchman, who gave the designs for Montagu House'. This cannot be the sculptor Pierre Puget, whose architecture is very different; the 'Monsieur Boujet' who signed Marot-esque drawings may be meant. Little more, however, is known of Boujet or Pouget, save that he was brought over from, and active in, France. At Het Loo and De Voorst, Marot collaborated with the Dutch architect Jacob Roman, who introduced the 'circular roof' to Holland in about 1680, and this raises yet another possibility in the attribution of the west front.

The ground plan (recorded as it was in the Duke's time in Laguerre's Grand Staircase murals) and the inventory taken in 1749/50 after his death show how the Proud Duke's Petworth was arranged along continental lines. The principal rooms of state were laid out, as today, in *enfilade* along the west front overlooking the front courtyard and the formal gardens beyond. To the north of the Marble Hall were the public apartments, including the Carved Room, an adjoining Tapestry Room, and a 'Picture Room next to ye North Cloisters' (the present Red Room). To the south of the Marble Hall was the Dining Room (Beauty Room) and the principal bedroom apartment (incorporating the present White and Gold Room and White Library), called the King of Spain's rooms after the visit in 1703 of the Archduke Charles of Austria, claimant to the Spanish throne. Adjacent, at the south end of the house, were the Duke and Duchess's separate private apartments; both provided a bedroom, with dressing-room and closet. Upstairs, looking west, were additional bedroom apartments for distinguished guests, as well as further family and senior servants' bedrooms. There were also first-floor North and South Galleries, various wardrobe rooms, the 'Bathing Room' (with an adjoining bedchamber to relax in afterwards) and a 'Stool Room' provided with a 'Water Hole ... Cistern and other Conveniences'.

The Franco-Dutch character of the Proud Duke's Petworth was carried through to the furniture and furnishings. The Duke's accounts reveal payments to prominent French and Dutch furniture makers and upholsterers, many of whom also worked for the Royal Household, such as Gerrit Jensen, Jean Poictevin, Pierre Pavie and the carver and gilder René Cousin. Among the purveyors of textiles was Sir William Gostlin 'His Majesty's Laceman'. Unfortunately, no surviving piece at Petworth can be identified with any of the furniture described in the bills, but the house still contains superb examples that can be attributed to makers mentioned in the

*Landscape with Jacob and Laban; by Claude, 1654
(no. 329; Somerset Room)*

accounts. The most magnificent piece of furniture of this period listed in the 1749/50 inventory was the state bed in the King of Spain's Bedchamber. From the description, 'Indian green & White Sattin laced with broad & narrow Silver Lace & 34 Silver Tassels', it must have been as sumptuous as the tall beds engraved by Marot, who is known to have provided 'a modell of the cornish' for a bed by Francis Lapiere at Boughton. Perhaps Marot and Poictevin collaborated at Petworth. 'Mr Podvin' and the otherwise unknown Robert Rhodes received £50 in 1687, 'besides £340 already paid'.

Like her friend Queen Mary, the Duchess of Somerset fell victim to the 'china-mania' that swept through the northern courts from the early seventeenth century onwards. The china was either Chinese or Japanese porcelain imported by the Dutch East India Company, or Dutch Delftware. The Duchess paid several Dutch and English dealers for china, including John van Collema, whose most prominent client was Queen Mary, while

Mrs Harrison (who also supplied the Queen) was paid £52 for a 'Jappan Cabinet and frame' in 1695. This may have been one of the 'India Cabinets' in the King of Spain's Drawing Room, each of which was surmounted by no fewer than '22 pieces of China'. Profusion was an essential feature of such displays, as is evident from contemporary engravings by Marot and others, and in the Duchess's Closet glass panels over the door and chimneypiece were 'ornamented wth carved work & 45 pieces of China'. The reflections in the glass would have multiplied the effect of massed groups of china, and it is interesting that Grinling Gibbons supplied carved giltwood mirrors (two of which still survive) over the doors and chimneypieces of the Queen's Gallery at Kensington Palace (1691), which was originally ornamented with porcelain by Queen Mary. Another connection with the Queen's method of displaying china is the set of carved walnut pedestals which still survives at Petworth. They were designed to display large covered jars of Chinese blue-and-white porcelain, which also remain in the collection. In England such stands survive only at Hampton Court and Petworth.

If Grinling Gibbons may have carved the Duchess's mirrors, he was certainly responsible for the carved surrounds to four full-length portraits and other carvings in the Carved Room. In its original guise, the Carved Room must have been all the more impressive for being half the size of the present room, which was extended by the 3rd Earl of Egremont in 1786–94. Gibbons's employment by the Duke of Somerset was almost certainly due to his previous work for the Crown, and also in the 1690s he worked at the Duke's old college, Trinity College, Cambridge, where he provided woodwork for Christopher Wren's Library, at the expense of the Duke, who was Chancellor of the University of Cambridge from 1689 until his death. Gibbons's statue of the Duke in the Wren Library (appropriately dressed as a Roman Emperor) commemorates his generosity to Trinity. The quality of the wood carving at Petworth is equalled only in Gibbons's *oeuvre* by the exquisite *trompe l'oeil* that he carved for the Grand Duke of Tuscany in 1682 (Uffizi, Florence), and a similar panel at Modena.

The Duke of Somerset collected pictures and sculpture. He was a friend of John, Lord Somers, a great collector of Italian drawings, and acquired 'a case of prints' in 1706. The Duke's signal purchase was the so-called 'Petworth Claude', the great *Landscape with Jacob and Laban* (no. 329; Somerset Room), which was painted in 1654 and imported into England after 1663. Due to be sold in 1686 at the Whitehall auction arranged by Grinling Gibbons and the frame-maker, restorer and auctioneer Parry Walton, it was subsequently bought by the Duke for £200. This was one of the first works by Claude to enter a British collection, and suggests the Duke's seriousness as a collector. He bought several other Old Masters at London auctions, and patronised such contemporary artists as Dahl, Closterman (who was also a dealer), Riley, Laguerre and Wootton. He also took care of the pictures he had inherited, employing Walton in 1689–90 for 'lineing, cleansing, priming and packing 11 of Vandykes Pictures'. Walton also supplied picture frames. In 1743 the diarist Jeremiah Milles noted 'on ye backstairs, some very good pictures, to which the Duke in his whimsys will not allow a better place'. Of one 'incomparable piece', Milles 'could not learn ye name of ye painter nor ye history: ye former I am told ye Duke studiously

The Duchess of Somerset is depicted riding on a triumphal chariot in Laguerre's murals on the Grand Staircase, 1718–20

conceals, as he does that of most of his pictures: out of an unusual and ridiculous whimsy.' The Duke's posthumous inventory reveals that he concentrated most of his pictures in what are now the Red Room and Oak Staircase.

As for sculpture, the Duke's most valuable acquisition was in 1691, when he paid £108 for the copy, probably by François Dieussart, of Michelangelo's so-called Sistine Madonna in St Peter's, Rome, now in the Chapel Passage, which had once belonged to the 14th Earl of Arundel, the greatest collector of sculpture in the reign of Charles I. The Duke also bought at least one piece of Antique sculpture: 'a Faustines head, Antient', which was acquired in 1683, and '8 Roman heads' were bought in 1694–5. He also probably purchased the two full-length Antique statues in the niches of the Marble Hall.

The Duke and Duchess of Somerset certainly succeeded in their aim of transforming Petworth into a seat worthy of their rank and fortune. Several royal visits are recorded, most notably that of Archduke Charles of Austria (to whom the Proud Duke presented a gold watch by Tompion), Prince George of Denmark and the great Duke of Marlborough. Prince George had taken seventeen hours to come down from London, his coach having overturned twice. The guests being assembled on 28 December 1703, there followed a series of formalities worthy of Versailles, involving visits to each other's suites with colourful retinues. Here, of course, the Proud Duke was in his element. He took a prominent part in the funerals of Charles II, Mary, William III, Anne and George I, and bore the orb at four coronations. He was Master of the Horse to Queen Anne and George I. His familiarity with courtly ceremonial seems to have coloured his more than ducal daily routine. In 1743 Jeremiah Milles recorded that:

The Duke spends most of his time here [ie at Petworth]: in grand retirement peculiar and agreeable only to himself. He comes down to breakfast at 8 of the clock in the morning in his full dress with his blue ribbon: after breakfast he goes into his offices, scolds and bullys his servants and steward till diner time, then very formally hands his Duchess downstairs. His table, tho spread in a grand manner as if company was expected always consists of his own family the Duchess and his 2 daughters and when he has a mind to be gracious the chaplain is admitted. He treats all his country neighbours and indeed everybody else with such uncommon pride, and desires that none of them visit him!

By this time, of course, he had long retired from public life, never in fact having regained his old position at court after 1715, when disgusted with the imprisonment of his son-in-law, Sir William Wyndham (father of one of the Duke's eventual heirs, the 2nd Earl of Egremont), on suspicion of Jacobitism, he instructed his servants to 'shoot all the rubbish' (ie his insignia as Master of the Horse) into the courtyard of St James's Palace. He was indeed far from servile as a courtier. In 1687, as Gentleman of the Bedchamber, he had lost his post but gained wide popularity for refusing James II's order to introduce the Papal Nuncio whom the Catholic James was determined to receive publicly at Windsor. Indeed, the Duke's political convictions stemmed from his Protestantism. He encouraged the advent of William and Mary, was rewarded by Queen Anne for his early and influential support, and as she lay dying, took steps to ensure the Hanoverian succession.

The Proud Duke died in 1748, and was outlived by his son, the 7th Duke, for only two years. A soldier, who had served with distinction under Marlborough, the 7th Duke (then Lord Hertford) had in 1713 married Frances Thynne, a Lady of the Bedchamber to Queen Caroline, who aspired to the patronage of learning, entertaining the poets Thomson and Shenstone at Alnwick, and writing spirited letters. On the 7th Duke's death without a surviving son, his property and titles were divided. His daughter, Lady Elizabeth Seymour, inherited the barony of Percy; her husband, Sir Hugh Smithson, became the Earl of Northumberland, master of Alnwick, Syon and Northumberland House, and in 1766 Duke of Northumberland. The 7th Duke's remote cousin, Sir Edward Seymour, succeeded to the dukedom of Somerset but to the smallest portion of the property. Petworth and the earldom of Egremont devolved upon the 7th Duke's nephew, Sir Charles Wyndham, 2nd Earl of Egremont.

CHAPTER SIX
THE 2ND EARL OF EGREMONT

The Wyndhams come originally from Norfolk (and are related to the Windhams of Felbrigg). In the sixteenth century one of the Norfolk Wyndhams married a cousin, of Orchard Wyndham in Somerset. In 1708 Sir William Wyndham, 3rd Bt, of Orchard Wyndham, married the Proud Duke's younger daughter, Katherine, and so it was that their son, Charles, inherited both the Egremont earldom and the Petworth estates on the death of his uncle, the 7th Duke of Somerset, in 1750.

Charles's father, Sir William, was a Tory, whose political career had flourished under Queen Anne, being appointed Secretary at War (1712) and Chancellor of the Exchequer (1713). After the Hanoverian succession in 1714, he was briefly imprisoned in 1715 for raising a rebellion in the West Country in support of the Stuarts. He was freed by the intervention of his father-in-law, the Proud Duke, but spent the rest of his time in Parliament in opposition to the Whig government of Sir Robert Walpole. His mentor in public and private life was Lord Bolingbroke, virtually Prime Minister in 1714, but who, as an attainted Jacobite, also never recovered his position after Queen Anne's death. Sir William Wyndham, like Bolingbroke, combined considerable abilities with a love of pleasure. Both characteristics were passed on to his son Charles.

Charles Wyndham, 2nd Earl of Egremont (1710–63), was first elected to Parliament (as a Tory, like his father) in 1725, but he came to prominence after his succession to the earldom, having by then allied himself with the Whigs. As 'the convert son of Sir William Wyndham', his political reputation increased to the point that in 1757 Earl Temple declared him destined to be another Pitt, whom

he succeeded in 1762 as Secretary of State for the Southern Department (effectively Foreign Secretary). His principal contribution to foreign policy was to stand firm against the Bourbon alliance of France and Spain. At home, after the Marquess of Bute's retirement in 1763, Egremont's brother-in-law George Grenville succeeded him as premier, and he, Egremont and Halifax (the other Secretary of State) formed a triumvirate which was broken only by Egremont's premature death in August 1763. Unlike his father, Egremont did not shine as an orator, but expressed himself admirably on paper. His French was impeccable: the drafting of one state paper was worthy of 'the duc de Choiseul [the then French Foreign Minister] in *politesse* and *franchise*'.

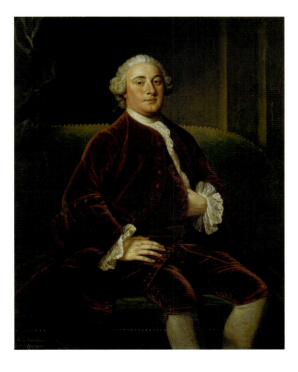

Charles Wyndham, 2nd Earl of Egremont; by William Hoare, 1763 (no. 538.)*

He had first visited France as a young Grand Tourist in 1729, and the lure of Paris and Parisiennes drew him back on several occasions. In 1736 the Francophile Lord Bolingbroke, in exile in France since 1715, extricated him from an entanglement with an actress. Egremont's enthusiasm for French style and culture was typical of the time, and is still evident at Petworth in the furniture and interior decoration that he commissioned, as well as in his activities as a collector of pictures and works of art, which are fundamental to Petworth's fame as a repository of the fine arts.

The goal of his Grand Tour in 1729–30 had, of course, been Italy, where he travelled in the company of the scholarly George Lyttelton, who was to become an equally distinguished builder, patron and collector at Hagley in Warwickshire. But Egremont's real aesthetic mentor was Thomas Coke, 1st Earl of Leicester (1697–1759). Indeed, Leicester's family seat, Holkham Hall in Norfolk, is the key to much of the activity at Petworth and at Egremont House, Piccadilly, during the 2nd Earl of Egremont's thirteen-year reign between 1750 and 1763. Designed by William Kent around 1730, Holkham was built (1734–64) as a setting for Leicester's Grand Tour collections, and, like Egremont House, was still unfinished on its owner's death. The executant architect of Holkham was a local man, Matthew Brettingham, and this explains Brettingham's employment by the 2nd Earl at Petworth and in the construction of Egremont House. Brettingham's sculpture galleries at Holkham and Petworth are still strikingly similar, despite the extension of the latter in the 1820s.

The craftsmen paid by Leicester also reappear in the 2nd Earl's accounts: Whittle and Norman, Vile and Cobb, Paul Saunders, George Bradshaw and William Hallett for furniture, picture frames, upholstery and tapestries; Maydwell and Windle for chandeliers and lustres; Thomas Bromwich for wallpapers; and Benjamin and Thomas Carter for chimneypieces. Brettingham's son, also Matthew, acted for both Leicester and Egremont as a purveyor of classical statuary. In partnership with the painter, archaeologist and dealer Gavin Hamilton, the younger Brettingham bought Antique statuary for Leicester between 1749 and 1754, and for Egremont between 1755 and 1763, thus creating two of the most important English collections to survive intact in their original settings (Petworth is the larger). If the sculpture formed an essential element of Holkham's interiors, so too did the pictures: 'I forgot to tell you', wrote Admiral Boscawen (the naval hero, an early patron of Robert Adam, and Egremont's fellow-guest at Holkham) to his wife in 1757, 'that Lord Leicester has a very fine collection of pictures, Lord Egremont who knows the hands and seems to understand them, says at least ten thousand pounds worth'.

The first entry in Egremont's accounts to refer to a work of art was in 1734/5: 'paid Mr Hogarth the Painter £4:4:0', although only two rather second-rate copies after Hogarth remain at Petworth. In 1740, the year of his father's death, the opening entry in his account book reveals that he had £1,220 4s 6d in ready money, from which he then paid £133 17s 6d 'for pictures and bronzes' at an auction. By 1741, he was buying 'tapestry fauteuils [armchairs] from Paris' and paying cabinetmakers and upholsterers such as Hallett and Bradshaw. At this time, he was making improvements at Witham, his country house in Somerset, and at his London house in Greek Street, which was fitted up by Bradshaw. His expenditure in the 1740s reveals, albeit on a smaller scale, the varied interests that he was later to be able to indulge to the full. As a member (from 1742) of the Dilettanti Society, founded in 1732 to prolong the civilised interests of those who had made the Grand Tour, he would have been abreast of the latest Italian developments in the antiquarian field. Payments for pictures (usually bought at auction or through dealers afterwards) and picture frames (by Gosset, Waters and Welbeloved) predominate, although there are payments to silversmiths (Willaume, de Lamerie and Archambo), to china dealers and gardeners, as well as to furniture-makers and upholsterers such as Paul Saunders.

After acceding to Petworth and the Egremont earldom in 1750, Charles could spread his wings. Indeed, his annual expenditure between October 1749 and December 1750 had already increased to £9,279, presumably in anticipation of his inheritance. The following year (1751) he spent the huge sum of £34,359 and until 1760 his annual outgoings were

£10,–18,000, with the exception of 1756–7 and 1757, when he spent £55,000 and £75,000, partly on his new London house. In 1751 he married Alicia Carpenter, a noted beauty and daughter of an Irish peer, Lord Carpenter. Having in 1750 paid £912 12s 4d 'for all the things at Petworth belonging to the late Duke of Somerset's estate', his first major expenses there seem to have been connected with the garden, for which he had a passion (see Chapter Two). 'Capability' Brown was first consulted at Petworth in 1751 and the following year he drew up his proposed design for the whole park.

The 2nd Earl was less radical in his treatment of the house. Apart from creating the North Gallery, his only other major alteration was the remodelling of the rococo White and Gold Room, probably between 1755 and 1761, when the Italian-Swiss *stuccadore* Francesco Vassalli was paid for plasterwork (presumably for the ceilings here and in the adjoining White Library, then the King of Spain's Bedchamber). The Bedchamber was hung with new crimson silk damask in 1756 *en suite* with the hangings of the magnificent rococo state bed, attributed to Whittle and Norman, and the upholstery of the gilt seat furniture (then parcel gilt to match the bed frame). Most of this furniture is now upstairs in Mrs Wyndham's Bedroom (the pier-glass is now the overmantel in the Square Dining Room), and replaced the Proud Duke's original Marot-esque furnishings.

As the 1764 inventory reveals, the 2nd Earl largely refurnished Petworth and from 1750 was actively employing cabinetmakers, upholsterers and upholders, chief among whom was the fashionable and expensive firm of Whittle and Norman. When their London warehouse burned down in 1759, shortly after Whittle's death, Lady Anson noted: 'Whittle and Co. must be undone: Lord Egremont has had a great loss'. The loss was probably furniture intended for Egremont's new London house, but partly due to his continued patronage, the firm recovered. One of the glories of Petworth is the series of huge rococo giltwood pier-glasses by Whittle and Norman, to whom payments were made in 1754–5, in 1757 and in 1759. In 1760–4 most of the furniture and furnishings of Egremont House were provided by Samuel Norman who claimed over £2,500 (and was paid about £1,700).

The undulating park landscape created by 'Capability' Brown for the 2nd Earl is shown in its maturity in Turner's Petworth, Sussex, the Seat of the Earl of Egremont: Dewy Morning, *1810 (no. 636; White Library)*

On the 7th Duke's death, Northumberland House had gone to the future Duke of Northumberland. The 2nd Earl of Egremont did not therefore inherit a town house with Petworth. His own house in Greek Street had presumably been given up, because he was leasing a house in Whitehall from the Duke of Richmond when, in 1756, he bought a plot of land and adjacent buildings at the western end of Piccadilly overlooking Green Park. Here, Egremont House still stands, behind its walled courtyard; it housed the Naval and Military Club (1865–1998). The new house, its plain Palladian façade in contrast to the riches within, was designed and built by Matthew Brettingham the Elder to provide intercommunicating rooms of parade for large numbers of guests and works of art around a domed central staircase.

Concurrently, Brettingham was instructed to provide a sculpture gallery at Petworth – presumably because space was short on the London site and the 2nd Earl was only just beginning to collect sculpture in 1756. Since the early seventeenth century, it had been common practice to concentrate pictures and sculpture in the capital where they could more readily be seen. The inventories taken in 1764 following the 2nd Earl's death reveal that Petworth contained only portraits

Giltwood pier glass and table (1755–1760) commissioned by the 2nd Earl and attributed to Whittle & Norman

and that Egremont House was the receptacle for over 200 Old Master pictures, including those inherited from the Northumberland collection. Most of them had, however, been purchased by the Earl himself. He bought at least one picture abroad, 'a little piece by Steenwyck', perhaps the *Christ with Nicodemus* (no. 242; Somerset Room), which was acquired in Brussels or Antwerp in 1752. In 1759 Matthew Brettingham the Younger sent him 'eight Small Pictures from Italy', including landscapes by Vanvitelli and Locatelli. The 'Picture Book' in which he listed his purchases reveals that ten other pictures came from Rome, including a Madonna by Conca. However, the great majority were bought on the burgeoning London art market, which was then beginning to challenge Amsterdam and Paris. He bought at the break-up of notable collections, including those of Sir Luke Schaub (1758), Dr Meade (1754) and at the initial sale in 1751 of pictures from the late Sir Robert Walpole's great collection at Houghton Hall, Norfolk, to which several visits by the 2nd Earl are recorded. His connoisseurship seems to have been greater than the norm, but he presumably received advice from men like John Anderson, who certainly worked for him as a picture restorer and go-between.

Horace Walpole linked Lord Egremont with a group of rich collectors whose 'glaring extravagance is the constant high price given for pictures' and 'who care not what they give'. The 2nd Earl's picture collection is one of the best documented of the mid-eighteenth century, and it is possible to establish that most of the prices were in fact reasonable. Jean Barbault's *Lady with a Rosary* (no. 520*; Egremont collection, White Library) cost under £5 in 1753; Ruisdael's *Waterfall* (no. 48*; Somerset Room) cost less than £10; Horst's *Boys at Play* (no. 572; Somerset Room) was £21, and in 1760 he paid £24 for a large landscape, then attributed to Cuyp, but which is probably the picture now given to Abraham van Calraet (no. 207; Beauty Room). More expensive were Bourdon's *Selling of Joseph* (no. 18; Red Room) at £99 in 1756, and Bril's *Landscape* (no. 83; Somerset Room), which cost £126 in 1754. The most expensive picture still in the collection is Teniers's *Archduke Leopold's Gallery* (no. 76; North Gallery) – £241 in 1756.

Sébastien Bourdon's Selling of Joseph *of c.1640 (no. 18.) was bought by the 2nd Earl in 1756*

The 2nd Earl's taste was typical of his time, apart from, for example, his comparatively expensive purchase at £48 of Jan Massys's *Card Players* (no. 47; North Gallery) and 'Two Large Murillios from Rotterdam' at just over £118 (when early Netherlandish and Spanish pictures were generally not in favour). He was also in the vanguard of a more sophisticated demand for Dutch pictures. The entries in his Picture Book, beginning in 1748/9, reveal that he bought 183 pictures during the last fifteen years of his life. The posthumous 1764 inventory of Egremont House reflects his priorities. Of the 220 pictures listed, 99 were Italian, 32 were Flemish, 35 Dutch, 24 French, 11 German, 2 Spanish, 7 English and 10 anonymous. Some were inherited, but the majority were the Earl's own purchases. The pictures were symmetrically arranged and hung from silk cords matching the crimson and blue Genoa damask wall-hangings, festoon curtains and upholstery. The 3rd Earl's sale in 1794 of Egremont House, most of its furniture and most of his father's pictures, broke up what was undoubtedly one of the most discriminating and beautifully arranged mid-eighteenth-century collections.

More extraordinary is the 2nd Earl's achievement as a collector of Antique sculpture. That his collection of some 70 statues and busts remains intact in the setting he built for it makes Petworth all the more remarkable. Antique sculpture was extremely expensive (the considerable cost of packing and transport had to be added to the purchase price) and its export was stringently controlled by the Papacy, which built up its own pre-eminent collections, still magnificently housed in the Papal

Museums within the Vatican. The Pope rarely gave licences for excavations within the Papal States, but certain dealers were allowed the privilege of digging in exchange for money and a share of the finds. It was also occasionally possible to acquire statues or other antiquities from the ancestral collections of the principal Italian families. At least one Italian collector, Cardinal Alessandro Albani, whose collections rivalled those of the Pope, was something of a *marchand amateur* (dealer-collector), both acquiring and dealing within a complex and sophisticated circle. At least one piece now at Petworth is known to have an Albani provenance (no. 18; North Gallery), and within Albani's orbit were the two men who put together the 2nd Earl's collection: the painter, archaeologist and dealer Gavin Hamilton and Matthew Brettingham the Younger, who regarded the 2nd Earl as their 'Patron and benefactor'. Their links with Albani were of paramount importance: not only did they find it easier to obtain papal licences for excavation and export, but they had access to the greatest expert of the day, Johann Winckelmann, who was Albani's librarian. They also employed experienced restorers of excavated fragments, including Pietro Pacilli (1716–73) and Bartolomeo Cavaceppi, whose published account of his work, the *Raccolta* (1768–72), includes engravings of two statues restored for 'Milord Egremont' still in the North Gallery (nos. 1 and 3). The restorers' skill lay in joining together Antique fragments with new elements to provide apparently complete figures, which would stand in symmetrical and harmonious ranks. At that time, English collectors 'had no value for statues *without heads*'.

The elder Brettingham's Petworth gallery was reminiscent of the long rectangular galleries of Roman *palazzi* and museums, with statues in niches, or on plinths, and busts mounted on brackets within roundels, or placed on consoles. It was formed by glazing an open cloister at the north end of the house. Such arcades or loggias were used as sculpture galleries by the ancient Romans and by their Italian successors. Its northern aspect was also entirely appropriate: Vitruvius himself had recommended a steady northern light as ideal for the display of pictures and other works of art, and this was repeated by later theorists. Brettingham's

name first appears in the 2nd Earl's accounts in 1753. The '7 large Sash frames with Circular heads' were paid for in October 1754, which must mean that the structure had been completed earlier that year.

The first mention of an antiquity was on 11 March 1755, when the 2nd Earl paid £21 10s 6d for an Antique bust of Isis at Dr Mead's sale. On 17 March Gavin Hamilton received £50 for an 'antique Bust of Venus' – almost certainly the 'Leconfield Aphrodite' (no. 73; Red Room). On 14 November Brettingham the Younger obtained the Earl's 'subscription for moulds of statues and busts' (the busts are now in the White and Old Libraries). By 1758 Hamilton's bill amounted to just over £400 and was slightly more in 1759. In 1760 the Earl laid out £315 for eleven busts from the Wimbledon collection of Lyde Brown, and £160 on four busts from Lord Dartmouth. The pattern of large payments to Hamilton (some £1,500 in 1760 and almost as much in 1762) continued until the Earl's death. Acquisitions were made from famous Roman collections (including several from the Palazzo Barberini), other pieces were restored following their excavation, and the niches on the southern wall of the North Gallery were still being filled ten years after the construction of the gallery. There was some further embellishment of the gallery in 1763, when 'moulding for Friezes, cornish etc' was supplied. The last shipment from Italy, which included a statue of Silenus, was made in 1765, two years after the death of the 2nd Earl.

The 1764 inventory reveals how the Antique sculpture was displayed, and indicates that the tradition that all of it remained in cases at the Earl's death is exaggerated. The gallery itself was filled both with full-length statues in the niches, and busts on brackets, apart from the two seated figures (nos. 15, 19), which were originally placed on plinths within niches at one end. There were four other rooms with concentrations of statuary: the Marble Hall with its '2 Large Marble Statues' still in the niches, the 'Oak Room' (Little Dining Room) and two ante-rooms (which no longer exist) giving off the Great Staircase. One of these, on the first floor, had large marble busts in recesses (as in the North Gallery) and over the doors. The placing of statuary in such hallways was in conscious emulation of ancient Roman and post-Renaissance Italian practice. Petworth was also distinctive, both in 1764 and subsequently, for the use of classical statuary as decoration throughout the house. In 1784, a traveller noted that 'all the principal apartments are furnished with antique statues and busts, some of which are of first rate value'. When the 2nd Earl placed an Antique bust upon a marble-topped pier-table, for example, it was often flanked by blue-and-white porcelain, with larger jars beneath and on either side of the table. These arrangements (recorded in the 1764 inventory) were untouched by the 3rd Earl, as watercolours by Turner and C. R. Leslie show.

The Antique statuary continued to excite comment long after the 2nd Earl's death, but a change in attitude can be detected even within the eighteenth century. A smoother, more refined style of restoration (in accordance with Neo-classical sculpture) became more acceptable. Already by 1776 a visitor to Petworth described the marbles as 'lamentably patched', an opinion reiterated in 1784 by G. A. Walpoole in *The New British Traveller*:

A singular circumstance attending them is, that a great many, when the late earl bought them, were complete invalids; some wanting heads, others hands, feet, noses etc. These mutilations his lordship endeavoured to supply, by the application of new members, very ill suited either in complexion or elegance of finishing, to the Roman and Grecian trunks, so that in some respects this stately fabric gives us the idea of a large hospital, or receptacle, for wounded and disabled statues.

The collection was expanded by the 3rd Earl, and although it was dismissed by Waagen in 1854 as 'of no high order, and chiefly restored works of the Roman time', it contains two Greek masterpieces (nos. 27, 73). Petworth is now of considerable rarity as the setting for the largest surviving eighteenth- and early nineteenth-century collection of Antique sculpture in a British country house.

The 2nd Earl's end was hastened by physical inertia and habitual over-indulgence. Horace Walpole recorded his demise at Egremont House on 21 August 1763:

Lord Egremont died suddenly, though everybody knew he would die suddenly: he used no exercise, and could not be kept from eating, without which prodigious bleedings did not suffice. A day or two before he died, he said, 'Well, I have but three turtle-dinners to come, and if I survive them I shall be immortal'. He was writing, as my lady breakfasted, complained of a violent pain in his head, asked twice if he did not look very particularly, grew speechless, and expired that evening.

'Agrippina as Ceres'; one of the Antique statues restored by Bartolomeo Cavaceppi for the 2nd Earl and illustrated in his Raccolta d'Antiche Statue, 1768–72. It is still displayed in the North Gallery (see p. 5)

CHAPTER SEVEN

THE 3RD EARL OF EGREMONT

George O'Brien Wyndham, 3rd Earl of Egremont (1751–1837) was a twelve-year-old schoolboy at Westminster when his father died, aged 53, in 1763. The 3rd Earl was, however, destined to be long-lived, and his death almost 75 years later ended what has been called Petworth's golden age. There are numerous accounts of his hospitality, his wit, his dislike of ceremony, his great abilities combined with a preference for a private life, his kindness and generosity to the poor, to children, and to the artists whom he encouraged. Egremont also shone as a benevolent landlord, an innovative farmer and as a breeder of racehorses, cattle and sheep. In 1798 Egremont characteristically refused the Presidency of the Board of Agriculture, but became increasingly famous for his experiments in crop rotation, in vegetable and fruit-growing, and in the development of planting tools such as the skim-coulter and the iron dibble. Hailed as 'one of the fathers of modern English agriculture', he also put money into forward-looking schemes: his investment in the Chichester canal and the Brighton chain-pier is commemorated in paintings by Turner. He had the local population inoculated against smallpox, erected or financed roads, waterways, hospitals, schools, almshouses, a gas works and Petworth Town Hall. 'It has been stated', wrote Mark Anthony Lower in 1865, 'that he spent in the course of sixty years in acts of charity and liberality, upwards of one million two hundred thousand pounds, or about £20,000 per annum'. His annual income was estimated at £100,000 and he owned over 110,000 acres in the west of England, Cumberland, Yorkshire, Ireland and West Sussex.

To the impecunious painter Benjamin Robert Haydon, Lord Egremont was 'like the Sun. The very flies at Petworth seem to know that there is room for their existence, that the windows are theirs.' As well as the regular gatherings of family, friends and artists, at 'that Princely seat of magnificent hospitality', as Haydon put it, there were tenants' and yeomanry dinners (in the Carved Room, North Gallery or Audit Room) and regal entertainments for the poor in the park. The greatest of these, when 6,000 were fed, waited on in medieval fashion by the local gentry, took place in May 1834. Witherington's painting of a summer fête in the park (no. 27*; Oak Stairs) depicts Lord Egremont reigning 'in the dispensation of happiness'. His *laissez-faire* benevolence surprised the traveller Louis Simond, used to the more exclusive attitudes of other landowners: 'He suffers the peasants of his village to play bowls and cricket on the lawn before the house; to scribble on the walls, and even on the glass of his windows.' Egremont liked people to come and go as they pleased, and Petworth was consequently like a great inn where after 'conferring the greatest favours, he was out of the room before there was time to thank him'.

In his youth, the 3rd Earl's reputation had been as a man of fashion whose chief interest according to the *Morning Herald* in 1782, was 'Street riding'. He made two Grand Tours (between 1770 and 1772), visiting Dresden, Berlin, Prague and Vienna as well as Venice and Paris. 'Voltaire and Rousseau were both alive . . .', he remembered of London society at the time, 'and their art and their doctrines engrossed the attention of everybody . . . Everything in fashionable life, dress, food, amusement, morals and manners all must be French . . . There was hardly a young lady of fashion who did not think it almost a stain on her reputation if she was not known to have cuckolded her husband.' He imported a Parisian courtesan, Mlle Du Thé, who appeared 'all bediamonded' at the opera. His liaison with Lady Melbourne reputedly produced one Prime Minister – the 2nd Viscount Melbourne – and the wife of another – Lady Palmerston, whose portrait by Lucas (no. 352) hangs in the North Gallery. He was a close friend of Charles James Fox, the leader of the Whig opposition, and paid his gambling debts and those of Georgiana, Duchess of Devonshire.

In July 1780 he proposed to Lady Maria Waldegrave, whose uncle, Horace Walpole, wrote of Egremont: 'He is eight-and-twenty, is handsome, and has between twenty and thirty thousand a year. You may imagine that he was not rejected by either mother or daughter.' However, the engagement was soon broken. To Walpole, Egremont was now 'a most worthless young fellow . . . as weak as irresolute . . . who by new indiscretion has brought universal odium upon himself.' The impediment was probably Lord Egremont's philandering and,

George O'Brien Wyndham, 3rd Earl of Egremont; a posthumous portrait by Thomas Phillips, showing him amid his collection in the North Gallery (no. 695; North Gallery)

perhaps, the realisation that he valued his freedom more than a respectable alliance. In about 1784 the fifteen-year-old Elizabeth Iliffe, or Ilive, became his principal mistress and the unofficial chatelaine of Petworth. She was the daughter of a Westminster schoolmaster, and bore Egremont seven children before their marriage in 1801. Mrs Wyndham, as she was known before her marriage, 'took great delight in painting', both as an artist and as a patron. The diarist Joseph Farington noted in 1798 that she planned to see the great Orléans collection of pictures then on exhibition in London following its purchase by a syndicate of English noblemen. She commissioned William Blake's *Last Judgement* (1808, no. 454; North Gallery), and was also an amateur scientist, setting up a private laboratory at Petworth.

Despite their happiness and shared artistic interests (only marriage provoked a separation due to his continued infidelities), the 3rd Earl pursued other *amours*, and even hung their portraits at Petworth, as Thomas Creevey noted with amusement in 1828, writing of 'my Lord's Seraglio'. Egremont's reputation as a womaniser convinced Lavinia, Countess Spencer that:

[he had] *forty-three* children who all live in the House with him and their respective Mothers; that the latter are usually kept in the background, but that when any quarrels arise, which few days pass without, each Mother takes part with her Progeny, bursts into the drawing room, fights with each other, Ld. E. and his Children, and I believe the Company, and make scenes worthy of Billingsgate or a Mad House.

Certainly, Creevey wrote of 'old Egremont's very numerous Stud', and he was very fond of children 'who always came away [from his dressing-room] with a sugar-plum, or some other little present'. To Lady Holland, who did not like 'to miss any opportunity of enjoying his society', Lord Egremont was a 'patriarch', whose house was 'a strange medley . . . artists and their wives and large numbers of their children'.

Most of the numerous and colourful accounts of staying at Petworth as a guest of the 3rd Earl date from towards the end of his life, when visiting artists were entranced by their kind reception. In 1798 arrangements had been more formal. According to

Witherington's painting (no. 27; North Gallery) depicts a summer fête in Petworth park in 1835, one of many such occasions laid on by the 3rd Earl*

Farington, when there was no company, the artists dined with Lord Egremont and Mrs Wyndham, but 'when company was expected they dined with Mrs Wyndham only'. Thomas Daniell, the painter of Indian landscapes, found Egremont 'good natured, but with much of the peer in him, the effect of a habit of authority'. Haydon, who had recently languished in a debtors' prison and whose sole rather unsatisfactory commission from Lord Egremont, *Alexander taming Bucephalus* (no. 660), hangs in the North Gallery, left perhaps the most telling description of Petworth in the 3rd Earl's day (in 1826):

He has placed me in one of the most magnificent bedrooms I ever saw! [hung with ancestral portraits on green damask] ... & a beautiful view of the Park out of the high window ... At breakfast, after the guests have all breakfasted, in walks Lord Egremont; first comes a grand child, whom he sends away happy. Outside the window moan a dozen black Spaniels, who are let in, & to them he distributes cakes & comfits, giving all equal shares. After chatting with one guest, & proposing some scheme of pleasure to others, his leathern gaters [sic] are buttoned on, & away he walks, leaving everybody to take care of themselves, with all that opulence & generosity can place at their disposal, entirely within their reach. At

dinner he meets everybody & then are recounted the feats of the day! All principal dishes he helps, never minding the trouble of carving! he eats heartily & helps liberally. There is plenty, but not absurd profusion – good wines, but not extravagant waste. Everything solid, liberal, rich and English.

Sophisticated guests were sometimes more critical. In 1823 the Hon. Edward Fox noted: 'The want of comforts, of regularity, and still more the total absence of clean linens, made it, splendid and beautiful as it is, far from being agreeable. Society too seems as little attended to as anything else. People of all descriptions, without any connections or acquaintance with each other, are gathered together and huddled up at the dinner table.' To Charles Greville, Lord Egremont 'lives with an abundant though not very refined hospitality. The house wants modern comforts, and the servants are rude and uncouth; but everything is good, and it all bears an air of solid and aristocratic grandeur.' In 1773 the Petworth servants' new liveries ('white jackets trimmed with muslin, and clean ones every two days') had struck Horace Walpole as the height of fashionable extravagance. By 1826, 'the liveries were extremely plain' (as was Egremont's own dress), but 'there were more [servants] in that house, of both sexes and in all departments, than in any House in England.' They kept their master's early hours. Creevey, asking for a glass of wine at 10.30pm, was told by the footman that 'the Butler *was gone to bed*', but he noted that 'in the morning they are at their posts with the Lark'.

The 3rd Earl made his first alterations at Petworth in 1774, when he commissioned Matthew Brettingham the Younger to convert the King of Spain's Bedchamber into the White Library. The bookshelves are still surmounted by plaster busts after the Antique, presumably from the moulds acquired by Brettingham when he was acting as the 2nd Earl's agent in Rome. Around 1777–8 the 3rd Earl modified the west front by taking down the Proud Duke's dome and statues. He also lowered the ground-floor windows to make it easier for his guests to step into the park. In 1794 he sold Egremont House and auctioned off most of his father's pictures at Christie's. He bought a smaller house at Grosvenor Place, but his mind was clearly turning to Petworth, where he was resuming his building activities with the enlargement of the Carved Room as a museum of the carvings by Gibbons and Selden, and the creation of the Square Dining Room and Somerset Rooms. In the 3rd Earl's

time all the principal rooms were painted white or red, and the curtains the length of the west front were of crimson or scarlet silk or moreen. Whereas his father had kept all his Old Masters in London, the mixture of paintings at Petworth now became more catholic, as his father's remaining pictures and the inherited Percy collections were expanded by the 3rd Earl's purchases and commissions. At Egremont's death, there were (and remain) more than 600 pictures in the collection, and his purchases of Antique sculpture and his sculptural patronage prompted the extension of the North Gallery between 1824 and 1827. The estate yard accounts are full of references to the continuous wanderings of this 'infinity of pictures and statues'. From 1791 men were continually 'taking down and putting up pictures in the house', making frames, providing stretchers and easels and constructing pedestals and plinths for statues. Pictures were also transported in packing cases to and fro between Petworth and London, often for exhibition at the Royal Academy and the British Institution.

In 1827 Thomas Creevey was amazed by 'the *immensity* of pictures on the ground floor of the House & as I was informed all the rooms above are full of them – then they are all mixed up together,

The Square Dining Room was created by the 3rd Earl; watercolour-gouache, c.1827; by J. M. W. Turner (Tate)

good and bad & Masters of all kinds & he [the 3rd Earl] is perpetually changing their places.' Turner's sketches of about the same date show that, despite the miscellany, the pictures were usually arranged symmetrically in well-balanced tiers. Creevey had been 'rather fidgetty in the morning to be about the house & after the pictures,' and had just started a tour before breakfast when 'old Egremont came *slouching* by':

'Pray, Lord Egremont, what is that curious picture . . .?' 'Ah!', says he, 'it is a devilish clever picture, is it not. Let's go look at it', and so we did . . . He slouched along the rooms with his hat on and his hands in his breeches pockets, making occasional observations upon the pictures and statues, which were always most agreeable and instructive, but so rambling and desultory, and walking on all the time, that it was quite provoking to pass so rapidly over such valuable materials.

As a patron, Egremont is most famous for his friendship with J. M. W. Turner, by whom there are no fewer than 20 paintings at Petworth. But he had been patronising the arts and fostering 'rising genius' long before he bought his first Turner, the so-called *Egremont Seapiece* (no. 33; North Gallery) probably at its Royal Academy exhibition in 1802 and certainly by 1805. For example, Egremont's name appears in an entry for 1783 in Sir Joshua Reynolds's ledgers; in 1785 he bought prints by Hogarth, and in 1795 commissioned a portrait of Mrs Wyndham and her children from George Romney, who had long had the 'ambition to place some work of his pencil in the princely mansion of Petworth'. Subject pictures by James Barry, Sir Francis Bourgeois, Henry Fuseli and John Opie may also have been acquired early in his collecting career. He was also one of only two aristocratic purchasers at the sale of Alderman Boydell's Shakespeare Gallery in 1805. However, it was from the 1790s that he flourished as a patron and collector of British art. His personal papers were apparently destroyed after his death, and his collecting activities have to be pieced together from a variety of other sources.

Petworth had already become a veritable academy by 1798, when the gem-engraver, Nathaniel Marchant, 'saw in the great Hall there, several pictures of Vandyke standing, and Collins, the Miniature painter, Phillips, the Portrait painter – and a Clergyman from Cambridge copying them – this was liberally allowed them to do by Lord Egremont'. The previous year, Romney had suggested that Thomas Hayley (a pupil of Flaxman) should 'pursue his professional studies in the gallery of his noble friend at Petworth' where, according to Haydon, he produced 'a small copy in clay' of a seated antique statue – presumably one of the two seated figures (nos. 15, 19), which were placed at one end of the then unextended North Gallery. Constable remembered of a visit to Petworth in 1834 that 'the Gainsborough [probably no. 106; North Gallery] was down when I was there. I placed it as it suited me, and I cannot think of it now without tears in my eyes.' Also in 1834 the painter C. R. Leslie was allowed to have 'a gem' by Bassano in his bedroom. There are three sketches by Turner of artists at work in the Old Library, still sometimes called 'Turner's Studio'. This huge room above the Chapel, with an immense east window, was ideal for the purpose, and was hung rather haphazardly with numerous pictures. In 1835, there were 55 – the usual Petworth mix of Old Masters and contemporary paintings, including works by Blake and Fuseli, and portraits by Hoppner and Beechey, who is probably depicted by Turner painting one of them here. When Turner had locked himself into his studio, only Lord Egremont was allowed to enter, but on one famous occasion Turner was fooled by his friend Sir Francis Chantrey's imitation of the Earl's 'peculiar step' and knock on the door.

Turner, Beechey, Chantrey, Phillips and Leslie were of the inner circle of Lord Egremont's artistic friends, and during their long stays were always made to feel at home. Chantrey and Phillips are known to have given advice on Egremont's 'projects in adorning his house', and it is likely that Turner's opinion was also sought. Egremont had bought several paintings by Turner between c.1802 and c.1813 (two being commissioned landscapes of Petworth and Cockermouth Castle), but the connection then lapsed until 1825. By 1828, three landscapes were already fixed in the Carved Room on trial, and the final four paintings – once again *in situ* in 2002 – were probably installed in 1830. These were given carved wooden frames in

The Lake in Petworth Park; by J. M. W. Turner, c.1828–30 (no. 142; Carved Room)

Gibbons-esque style by Jonathan Ritson, a carver who was employed for over eighteen years to provide additional carvings for the room. Two of Turner's Carved Room paintings are depictions of Petworth park, which also inspired numerous sketches in gouache and watercolour. Over a hundred and twenty sheets of light blue paper (Tate) reveal Turner's private reactions to Petworth's interiors and landscape. Painted *c.*1827, they are among Turner's most beautiful and immediate works, ranging from the sketchiest shorthand note of a single figure or of the effect of changing light in the park to more detailed studies of views and interiors. Since 1991 the more finished sketches – those of the Square Dining Room, North Gallery and Red Room in particular – have informed the re-creation of picture-hangs and schemes of decoration admired by Turner. Seeing Petworth through Turner's eyes is therefore becoming increasingly possible in reality.

In 1834 Turner's great contemporary, John Constable, was also a guest of Lord Egremont, who 'ordered one of his carriages to be ready every day, to enable Constable to see as much of the neighbourhood as possible'. According to his friend and fellow guest, C. R. Leslie, Constable 'filled a large book with sketches in pencil and watercolours, some of which he finished very highly ... He rose early, and had often made some beautiful sketch in the park before breakfast ... His dressing table was covered with flowers, feathers of birds, and pieces of bark with lichens adhering to them which he had brought home for the sake of their beautiful tints.' Constable declared: 'Claude nor Ruysdael could not do a thousandth part of what nature here represents', but his failure to receive a commission from Lord Egremont led him, incorrectly, to assume that 'landscape affords him no interest whatever'.

'On matters of art', wrote Leslie, 'Lord Egremont thought for himself; and his remarks were worth remembering. He said to me: "I look upon Raphael and Hogarth as the two greatest painters that ever lived".' His tastes were catholic and he bought Old Masters and Antique sculpture as well as commissioning portraits, landscapes and historical works. His prime concern was to encourage study and to commission works of inspiration rather than of imitation, telling Leslie: 'I wish to keep you employed on such [historical and literary] subjects instead of portraits.' The North Gallery is filled with pictures and sculpture in tune with Egremont's literary tastes. Works inspired by Shakespeare, Chaucer, Spenser, Milton, Swift,

87

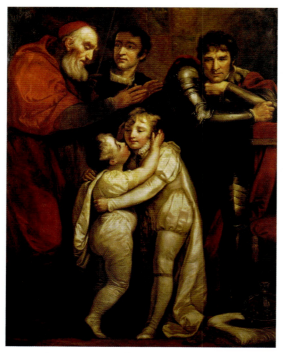

Richard III and the Little Princes; by James Northcote (no. 92; North Gallery). One of many literary subjects commissioned from contemporary artists by the 3rd Earl

Thomson, Prior, Beattie, Horace and Cervantes, by a litany of British artists including Reynolds, Turner, Fuseli, Opie, Clint, Northcote, Thomson, Leslie, Blake, Flaxman, Rossi and Westmacott, are placed alongside biblical, mythological and historical subjects by many of those painters and sculptors, as well as Carew, Nollekens, Haydon and Phillips. The gallery also contains Old Masters, portraits and landscapes, as it did in 1835, when Turner's landscapes were confined to it and the Carved Room.

If the 3rd Earl's patronage of historical painting was enlightened at a time when, in Haydon's words, it was 'not yet taken up as it should be in a wealthy country like England', his sculptural commissions were quite exceptional. Most contemporary English patrons of sculpture favoured the Italians, and Canova in particular. In 1819, on an incognito visit to Chantrey's studio, Lord Egremont asked him whether he had ever departed from portraiture

by modelling 'an ideal subject, or anything from poetry'. Chantrey replied: 'Our patrons do not give commissions for such subjects, at least not to English artists; the only sculptor among us who has been employed on anything of the kind is Flaxman, who has a commission from Lord Egremont.' The 3rd Earl owned two works by Flaxman, including a masterpiece, the *St Michael overcoming Satan* (c.1817–26, the subject taken from Milton's *Paradise Lost*), around which the North or Square Bay of the North Gallery was built in 1826–7. Apart from St Michael's spear, it was carved from a single block of marble at a cost of £3,500, and according to the 3rd Earl's inscription on the base, 'Flaxman's achievement was hardly surpassed by the most celebrated productions of ancient times, and certainly by none of his own'.

Two other important compositions suggested by poetry are *Celadon and Amelia* (c.1820; no. 105; South Corridor, North Gallery), by J. C. F. Rossi, the dramatic subject taken from Thomson's *Seasons*, and a bas-relief, *Horace's Dream*, inspired by Horace's *Ode to Calliope* (exhibited and 'just completed' in 1823; no. 111) by Sir Richard Westmacott, who personally installed it in the wall at the west end of the North Gallery. Westmacott, nicknamed 'Westmacotteles' by Egremont because of his addiction to all things Greek, was a regular visitor to Petworth in the 1820s, and probably advised his host on matters of display, given his responsibility for the presentation of sculpture at the British Museum.

The influence of Canova is evident in Westmacott's *Nymph and Cupid* (exhibited 1827; no. 98) and perhaps also in Rossi's *British Athlete* (exhibited 1828; no. 99), which is reminiscent of Canova's *Pugilists* in the Vatican. Rossi's plea for more money in 1826, while working on this statue, for once failed to arouse Lord Egremont's sympathy: 'Rossi, I suppose, applied in the style of a butcher', concluded Haydon with satisfaction (Rossi had been his landlord). Other sculptors commissioned by the 3rd Earl included George Garrard and Joseph Nollekens. That the Earl also bought Nollekens's plaster *Seated Venus* at his posthumous studio sale in 1823, and commissioned a marble copy of it by Rossi's assistant, Richard Williams, indicates his regard for this distinguished sculptor of a previous generation. It also suggests that he was consciously compiling a representative collection of contemporary British sculpture.

Egremont encouraged Sir Francis Chantrey to turn away from his habitual portraits to produce an ideal work: 'a capital figure of Satan, with something of his original brightness'. This project 'was destined to tease the sculptor, more or less, as long as he lived. He knew that expectation had been raised, and he felt at once the difficulties of the task, and the peril – or rather the certainty of failure', wrote Chantrey's biographer in 1851. A young Irish sculptor, John Edward Carew, had no such qualms, and having come to Lord Egremont's notice in 1813, was almost exclusively employed by him from about 1820. A former assistant of Westmacott, he was praised by Haydon in 1826 as 'perhaps the best cutter of marble in England ... as rapid as lightening [sic] with his chisel, but idle in thought, preferring the chat of a gossiping Coffee House to the glory of fame'! His 'light spirits', 'gay mind' and his Irish charm certainly appealed to Lord Egremont, who found that Carew's 'Genius and Conception' was in tune with his own taste for 'colossal works of heroic size'. Egremont not only gave him subjects to illustrate, but closely followed their progress, cancelling more than one commission when well advanced. Carew was later to criticise what he called his patron's 'capricious and sudden' changes of heart. Until 1831, Carew remained in London, producing there an *Adonis* (1823–5/6; no. 100) and the great group of *Venus, Vulcan and Cupid* (c.1827/8–31; no. 115), for which he received £4,000 (£500 more than Flaxman for his slightly smaller *St Michael*). These were placed in the North Gallery, to which, after its completion in 1827, Egremont intended further alterations to be made under Carew's direction. Due to a severe illness, however, Lord Egremont put a stop to these plans.

From 1832 to 1837 Carew lived near Petworth and was also provided with a studio at Brighton, where Egremont had a house. In the final year of his life, the 3rd Earl, ever eager to be building, was constructing 'a new dining room for the tenants' [the present tea-room]. 'At the time,' remembered Carew, 'I was working on a large group of Prometheus; and after moving it into this new hall, Lord Egremont called it the "Promethean Hall".' This was the colossal group (no. 116) now in the North Gallery, from which the 3rd Earl had moved Carew's *Venus, Vulcan and Cupid* to stand at the opposite end of the Promethean Gallery. This second gallery, doubling as a tenants' hall and incongruously hung with cattle pictures, was clearly intended as a museum of Carew's sculpture, but the enterprise was curtailed by the 3rd Earl's death. The Square Bay of the North Gallery now contains almost all of Carew's commissioned sculpture.

Carew's insolvency led him to sue Lord Egremont's executors for the astonishing sum of £50,000, despite the lavish payments that he had received during Lord Egremont's lifetime. The published proceedings of the ensuing court case (1841–2), in which Westmacott and Chantrey appeared as expert witnesses, is an important document not only for Carew's relationship with his patron but for its rarity as a record of sculptural practice in early nineteenth-century England. Carew's claim was rejected, and his bankruptcy ten years later confirmed the 3rd Earl's prediction: 'you will come to the dogs'.

The 3rd Earl's open-handed hospitality gave Petworth the character of a luxurious academy, where Turner and Constable could be equally inspired by the Proud Duke's 'grand and solemn' Claude, or by the natural beauty of the park. To Leslie, Lord Egremont was 'the most magnificent, and at the same time the least ostentatious nobleman in England'. He disliked 'ribbons and higher titles' and his refusal of the Garter was typical. His multifarious activities encompassed the arts and sciences. To Creevey, he was 'as extraordinary a person, perhaps as any in England; certainly the most so of his own caste or order'. On hearing of his death, Charles Greville concluded that 'his death will be more felt within the sphere of his influence ... than any individual's ever was'. Leslie described his funeral in Petworth parish church in November 1837:

All the shops in the town were closed, and business entirely suspended. Indeed all the inhabitants were present, either following the procession, or lining the way as it passed. There was not a single carriage. All the mourners followed the coffin on foot, and the line was continued to a great length. The many artists who had enjoyed his patronage, Turner, Phillips, Carew, Clint, and myself, were present.

CHAPTER EIGHT
MODERN TIMES

The 3rd Earl's eldest son, George (1787–1869), inherited his father's possessions but could not inherit his titles due to his illegitimacy. The earldom (and the Orchard Wyndham and Devon estates) devolved upon the 3rd Earl's nephew, and became extinct on the latter's death in 1845. George Wyndham was known as Colonel Wyndham after 1830, when he was appointed Colonel of the 24th Foot, and in 1859 he was created Lord Leconfield, the name of a Percy fortress and estate in Yorkshire which came into the family in the fourteenth century. Like his father, he was a keen sportsman, and he and his younger brother, Henry, both kept packs of hounds. After their father's death, the brothers fell out over the demarcation of their hunting countries, which led to a long and bitter feud. According to their great-grandson, John Wyndham:

George was shy, taciturn and solitary – traits which he had inherited from his father without his father's sensibility. Perhaps their bastardy had given him and Henry chips on their shoulders. Anyway, they both had vile tempers. Neither brother was an intelligent or cultivated man. George's affections were strong though not diffuse: they embraced his wife, his children and the chase.

Henry had distinguished himself at the Battle of Vittoria in 1813, where he captured the fleeing King Joseph Bonaparte's carriage, which was filled with over 200 rolled-up Old Masters looted from Spanish collections (many now at Apsley House, London), and at Waterloo. This explains his father's choice of subjects for the battle pictures in the Beauty Room, the Petworth shrine to Napoleon.

The 1st Lord Leconfield's management of Petworth was exemplary and conservative. Charles Barry submitted an estimate for a 'New approach and Entrance on the East Side' in 1839, but they were not executed. Lord Leconfield completed his father's scheme for the Carved Room, continuing to employ Jonathan Ritson until 1846. He had the paintings numbered, the hang of pictures throughout the house recorded, and a basic printed catalogue was published in 1856. In 1854 he had pictures varnished and in 1856 they were cleaned by H. R. Bolton, who had drawn up illustrated lists in 1847. The house was extensively repaired, but there were few alterations.

When Lord Leconfield's daughter-in-law, Constance, wife of Henry, 2nd Lord Leconfield, came to Petworth in 1867, after their honeymoon at Uppark, she found that remarkably little had changed since the 3rd Earl's death in 1837. Lord Leconfield she described as a shy and affectionate man of 80 who still followed his hounds in a brougham and who 'had what is called the "Wyndham temper", and he used very forcible language at times'. According to his third son, Percy, he had a deep love and understanding of the country and of agriculture, 'his keen common sense going to the root of everything'. His adored wife, Mary, was 'deeply religious, of the pronounced Evangelical type' and was 'also very strict as to conventions, and what she considered due to her position as mistress of Petworth. No familiar intercourse was allowed with the town, the children and servants were forbidden to go into it, and she herself never entered it except in a carriage'. The carriage and horses accompanied her on the train to London, and as Lady Leconfield would not 'travel with strangers ... the upper servants at Petworth always travelled first class and filled the vacant seats in her compartment'. The Petworth housekeeper was Mrs Smith, who served the family for over 30 years, and who, after Lady Leconfield's death in 1863, ensured that her late mistress's rules were observed:

No maid was allowed to go into the town, their dress was most severely regulated, no hat could be allowed in church on Sundays ... attendance at church was strictly enforced, and the whole household sat in the gallery in pairs rising in tiers behind the family seats. When some experts came down to view the pictures, and expressed opinions as to their genuineness: 'How should they know more than the late Lady Leconfield?' said Mrs Smith, and to her that settled the matter.

After his wife's death, Lord Leconfield lived a retired life, and 'never again asked a stranger into Petworth House'. His occupation of the Marble Hall as a cluttered and carpeted study is recorded in a view painted about 1865 by his daughter-in-law, Madeline, wife of his favourite son, Percy (no. 704; Marble Hall). The Percy Wyndhams used to spend most of the winter at Petworth with their three children, their nurse and nurserymaid.

The 1st Lord Leconfield's death in 1869 ushered in a decade of considerable changes to Petworth. The fashionable architect Anthony Salvin was immediately commissioned by Henry, 2nd Lord Leconfield to undertake major alterations at the south end of the house (which had always been the family's domestic quarters). The carriage drive from the west was now diverted from the Marble Hall, and led via iron gates (copies of Tijou's gates at Hampton Court) to a new main entrance on the east or town side. Salvin screened off the south end from the servants' block and courtyard (the Fountain Court), from which the 3rd Earl's fountain was removed to enliven the private garden. The real tennis court enclosing the north end of the old Fountain Court was demolished (it was rebuilt in its present position next to the estate yard) and the view to the Pleasure Ground opened up. New stables were built creating an enlarged stable courtyard, while preserving the eighteenth-century stable range, and the Church Lodge (the town entrance) was erected alongside. The most radical alteration to the principal rooms was the remodelling of the 3rd Earl's enlarged Carved Room. Here Salvin's builders, Charles Smith of 44 Upper Baker Street, London, removed the 3rd Earl's grey-white paint from panelling and doors, so that Gibbons's and Selden's carvings were seen, as originally, upon a darker oak background. Most of Ritson's carvings were removed, as were the landscapes by Turner, and the dado and fireplaces were altered. The 2nd Lord Leconfield also removed paint from seventeenth-century carvings and doors in the Little Dining Room, and repainted several other rooms, including the Marble Hall, North Gallery and Square Dining Room. Percy and Madeline Wyndham were both in the vanguard of the Arts and Crafts movement, commissioning Philip Webb in 1881 to build Clouds, near Salisbury, Wiltshire, the epitome of an Arts and Crafts country house. This must explain why Morris & Co. was employed

The Marble Hall in the 1860s, when it was used by the 1st Lord Leconfield as a study; watercolour by Madeline Wyndham (no. 704; Marble Hall)

by the 2nd and 3rd Lords Leconfield to provide wallpapers, damask wall-coverings, upholstery, curtains, carpets and lamps for Petworth, including some extremely rare printed velvets.

Constance Leconfield (who noted that 'Morris cretonnes' became fashionable in the 1870s) and her sister-in-law Madeline were close friends who both insisted that their husbands should make up an earlier quarrel which blew up 'over the port and their inheritance'. The younger brother, Percy, had been treated extremely generously in his father's will, which allowed him to commission the building of Clouds. The truce was ratified by an invitation to Clouds, where Lord Leconfield was bitten in the hall by Percy's dog and spent the night worrying whether he was going to get rabies. This annoyed Constance Leconfield's elder brother, Lord Rosebery, then Prime Minister, 'who resented other people in his circle being as neurotic as he was'.

The 2nd Lord Leconfield's building activities extended to London where he gave up the 3rd Earl's house in Grosvenor Place and built Leconfield House in Chesterfield Gardens, Mayfair. Again, Salvin was his architect, although the building was completed after 1879 by Thomas Henry Wyatt. Lord Leconfield 'had barrels of drinking-water sent up from Petworth. He always said that he was not going to risk his children catching typhoid fever from drinking the London water.' The 'mad business' of carting water from Petworth to London ended with the death at Petworth on 13 January 1895 of Lord Leconfield's son, George, from typhoid.

The 2nd Lord Leconfield inherited his family's love of field sports – a letter from Scotland to his wife at Petworth read: 'I have killed only 8 fish & lost 12 that were at the point of death. Thine, Henry. PS I enclose a fish.' He was also interested in the arts, not only as a builder, for he added highly important French furniture sold at the Hamilton Palace sale in 1882, most notably a commode made by Boulle (Red Room). According to his grandson, he was:

Handsome and grand
And idolised land.

The 4th Lord Ribblesdale summarised his character: 'He hardly ever spoke in the House, but his idol was Land in all its complexions and aspects. Cool, critical and shrewd, looking on the personal administration of great estates in Ireland and England as a profession, I can understand his being an awkward customer for a permanent official or a Minister. ... On Land he spoke from practical contact and knowledge, with authority.' According to *The Complete Peerage*, he owned a total of 109,935 acres, worth £88,112 a year in 1883. He resented the fact that his father's bastardy had prevented him being an earl, but when an earldom was offered by Queen Victoria in 1886, he refused it, and afterwards 'was never quite the same'.

He died, after a long illness, in London in 1901 (his widow, Constance, lived on until 1939) and was succeeded by his second son, Charles, whose long life connects the reign of Queen Victoria with the gift of Petworth to the National Trust in 1947. As a lieutenant in the 1st Life Guards, he was wounded in the South African War (1899–1902) and served in the First World War (as did his four younger brothers, one of whom was killed in action in 1914). In 1913, two years after their marriage, he and his wife Violet were painted by de Laszlo. Lord Leconfield's fashionable and punctilious dress in the portrait reveals the formal side of his character: his nephew and heir, John Wyndham, remembered that in the later 1930s:

We had to dine in white tie and tails. When a gentleman came to stay with only a dinner jacket, and apologised for not having brought his tail-coat, Uncle Charles would offer what he thought the sage advice: 'You should sack your man'. It never entered his head that some of his guests might not have valets.

His nephew thought him 'the kindest of men', but 'taciturn and gruff'. He was 'a great though morose trencherman', and 'ate so much that, after consultation with his physicians, he decided to restrict himself to huge breakfasts and huge dinners ... A baked egg and a glass of Madeira became his rule at luncheon. By the evening, quite ravenous, he would wander about the great house from room to room, staring out of rather bulbous eyes at his guests (if any), but saying nothing.'

Charles, 3rd Lord Leconfield, and his wife Violet (centre left and right) at a hunt meet at Petworth

The most unfortunate incidents during his reign of over 50 years were the sale (which he later regretted) of thirteen important paintings in 1927, and the disastrous 'restoration' of several others in the late 1920s and 1931 (thereafter he never allowed any of the pictures to be touched). The sale was engineered by a dealer masquerading as a hunting colonel who profited from the huge demand in America for Old Masters, especially those with distinguished provenances. The pictures included two Rembrandts, a Frans Hals, Holbein's portrait of Derich Berck and a Watteau. Several are now in the Metropolitan Museum of Art, New York, but a Bronzino portrait has recently been retrieved for Petworth by the family.

In February 1947 James Lees-Milne, the National Trust's Historic Buildings Secretary, recorded a vignette of Petworth just emerging from its wartime chrysalis, occupied by the solitary Lord Leconfield and a skeleton staff:

We lunched together (I not sent to the servants' hall). A large meal was left for us on hot stoves in the small dining-room. His kitchen is in the building over the way and his food has to pass underground. Promptly at 1.30 he summoned the nice old housekeeper and Moss, the house-carpenter, to take me round the house. All the pictures are now re-hung but the state-rooms are still under dust-sheets. Furniture in splendid condition, smelling of mansion polish and camphor. The housekeeper has one couple, the stableman and wife, who work in the house from 6.30 am to midday. Lord Leconfield joined us upstairs and waddled around. We made an odd little party. He is sweet with the servants, jokes with them in his funny, ponderous way. They however curiously subservient and rather sycophantic.

The future of Petworth and its collections greatly exercised the mind of Lord Leconfield's heir, his nephew John Wyndham, whose elder brother, Henry, was killed at El Alamein in 1942. John Wyndham had spent the war as Harold Macmillan's right-hand man at the Ministry of Supply, the Colonial Office, in the Mediterranean and at the Air Ministry, and their connection was resumed in 1957, when Macmillan, by now Prime Minister, invited him to become his private secretary. John Wyndham's first-hand experience of Whitehall stood him in good stead during his frustrating negotiations with the Treasury over Petworth. Given the uncertain future for great houses, John

Wyndham's first concern was to persuade Lord Leconfield of the advantages of the National Trust as Petworth's custodian:

Before my uncle died I had pressed him to give Petworth and its park to the National Trust. I wanted to make sure that Petworth was preserved, and who could tell what the future might hold? I put this to Uncle Charles, and it was certainly one of the bravest things I've ever done. He could have struck me out of his will. Happily he didn't. But when he died [in 1952] I was faced with heavy death duties. Petworth House (and the park but not the estate) had already been given to the National Trust [in 1947] with the huge endowment sum of £300,000. It now occurred to me that some of the 700 pictures in the house might also be handed over in lieu of death duty, to remain on the walls where they belonged as the property of the nation.

John Wyndham, 1st Lord Egremont, who masterminded the complex negotiations that brought Petworth and a large proportion of its contents to the National Trust: Osbert Lancaster's portrait was used on the dust-jacket of Wyndham's autobiography, Wyndham and Children First, *1968*

John Wyndham's idea is now an accepted procedure, but because this was the first time it had been mooted, the negotiations were protracted. He began by writing a personal letter to the then Chancellor, R. A. Butler: 'There is no collection quite like it anywhere in the world today; and it oughtn't to be dispersed.' Butler applauded 'the imaginative offer', explained that an in lieu scheme was already under consideration, and John Wyndham went ahead:

Oh, what a mistake! I was the guinea-pig for the new plan. The plan was all right in principle: the Treasury would take over the stuff in lieu of death duties and arrange for the Trust to manage it. But the trouble and difficulty was arriving at a fair price, for the Treasury had not been directly in the art market before.

Another problem was that the government's expert advisers (the National Gallery for pictures) could not understand the Trust's desire to accept furnishing pictures of secondary importance but historical value. In the end, there was stalemate, and the situation was saved only by John Wyndham's altruism in accepting the Treasury's net offer of £553,148: 'I had been hoping for a million pounds', he wrote: 'Whatever happens to me or my family, Petworth House, its contents and its park should be preserved for posterity. I am glad.'

The Treasury's valuation was considered grossly unfair by Sir Anthony Blunt, Surveyor of the Queen's Pictures, who was involved in the negotiations on the Trust's behalf. As the Trust's Honorary Adviser on Paintings, he had already been responsible for a complete rearrangement of the pictures and had organised conservation work. Blunt's campaign began in 1952 after Lord Leconfield's death, and before the house was opened to the public. While eschewing 'a museum atmosphere', pictures were now arranged by subject – Van Dycks in the Square Dining Room, Turners in the 'Turner Room' (as it then became known) – and the 3rd Earl's miscellaneous arrangements ('a mixed bag', as Blunt put it), which had survived in several rooms, were unwittingly dismantled. To be fair to Blunt, he was unaware of the history of the collection's previous deployment; there had indeed been alterations since the 3rd Earl's death, and his brief from the Trust was

The Red Room, after it had been rehung by Anthony Blunt with most of the Petworth Turners on a yellow silk

simply to 'see whether anything needed to be done about rehanging and cleaning'. In retrospect, he realised that he had broken with Petworth tradition 'to keep as far as possible the hanging arranged by the Third Earl'. But he did so with the blessing of the family, a fundamental principle of the Trust's management of its collections.

Times change, and since 1987 the present Lord and Lady Egremont have made generous loans of pictures to the Trust, to make it possible for the spirit of the 3rd Earl's crowded picture-hangs to be re-created. Once again, as in the Square Dining Room, the visitor can appreciate Petworth's interiors as Turner painted them, and in the North Gallery Turner's landscapes can be seen not only top-lit on a red ground, as he intended, but in relation to paintings by his contemporaries. In the 1950s the Trust had also redecorated most of the public rooms without reference to their historic treatment, and this approach is also gradually being reversed to restore the original nineteenth-century or earlier schemes. The public rooms had become rather bare and formal after the 1950s, and again with the family's help, additional contents have been brought in to increase both the sense of grandeur and of domesticity. Lord and Lady Egremont have lent superb silver for the Square Dining Room, as well as the huge copper *batterie de cuisine* for the newly opened Kitchen in the Servants' Quarters. A set of bedrooms, furnished and used by the family, has been open on weekdays since 1987. The work of redecoration and rearrangement has been made possible by an anonymous donation from a generous benefactor of the Trust, and other generous donations – the restoration of the Carved Room (completed 2002) marks a high point in a decade of work which has been undertaken by the National Trust in partnership with Lord and Lady Egremont. The improvement of the interior could only begin after twenty years of roof repairs (grant-aided by English Heritage). Recent building works rectified the structural instability of the first floor where huge timbers had been virtually eaten away by boring insects. The repair of the west front will follow.

In 1963, after six years as Harold Macmillan's private secretary, John Wyndham was created 1st Lord Egremont, and in 1967 he succeeded his father as 6th Lord Leconfield. His memoir of Petworth and of his own career, *Wyndham and Children First* (1968), records his years with Macmillan, whose 'Motto for Private Office and Cabinet' was 'Quiet, calm deliberation disentangles every knot'. In 1972 his eldest son, Max, a biographer and novelist, succeeded him as 2nd Lord Egremont and 7th Lord Leconfield. Lord Egremont and his family continue the 800-year-old tradition of residence at Petworth.

BIBLIOGRAPHY

The Egremont Papers are administered by the West Sussex Record Office (three volumes of a catalogue have been published). An entire issue of *Apollo* (cv, no. 183, May 1977) was devoted to Petworth, with articles on the building, sculpture, furniture, paintings, garden and park.

BATHO, G.R., 'The Percies at Petworth, 1574–1632', *Sussex Archaeological Collections*, xcv, 1957, pp. 1–27.

BATHO, G.R., 'Notes and Documents on Petworth House, 1574–1632', *Sussex Archaeological Collections*, xcvi, 1958, pp. 108–34.

BATHO, G.R., *The Household Papers of Henry Percy, Ninth Earl of Northumberland (1564–1632)*, Royal Historical Society, 1962.

BLUNT, Anthony, 'Petworth Rehung', *National Trust Studies*, 1980, pp. 119–32.

BUTLIN, Martin, Mollie LUTHER and Ian WARRELL, *Turner at Petworth: Painter and Patron*, London, 1989.

COLLINS-BAKER, C.H., *Catalogue of the Petworth Collection of Pictures in the Possession of Lord Leconfield*, London, 1920.

EGREMONT, Lord [John Wyndham], *Wyndham and Children First*, London, 1968.

EGREMONT, Max, 'The Third Earl of Egremont and his Friends', *Apollo*, cxxii, October 1985, pp. 280–7.

FONBLANQUE, E.B. de, *Annals of the House of Percy*, London, 1887, 2 vols.

GORE, F. St J. Gore, 'Old Masters at Petworth' in *The Fashioning and Functioning of the British Country House*, G. Jackson-Stops ed., Studies in the History of Art 25, National Gallery of Art, Washington, 1989, pp. 121–31.

HUSSEY, Christopher, *The Story of Petworth House: Its Owners, Its Contents*, 1926 [reprinted from *Country Life* articles, 28 November, 5, 12, 19 December 1925, and 13 February 1926].

HUSSEY, Christopher, 'Petworth House, Sussex', *Country Life*, 7 March 1947, pp. 422–5.

JACKSON-STOPS, Gervase, 'Petworth and the Proud Duke', *Country Life*, 28 June 1973, pp. 1870–4.

JACKSON-STOPS, Gervase, 'Wilderness to Pleasure Ground', *Country Life*, 26 June 1975, pp. 1686–7.

JACKSON-STOPS, Gervase, 'Bordering on Works of Art' and 'Great Carvings for a Connoisseur': 'Picture Frames at Petworth – I, II', *Country Life*, 4, 25 September 1980, pp. 798–9, 1032–3.

LAING, Alastair, *In Trust for the Nation*, exh. cat., The National Gallery, London, 1995.

LECONFIELD, Constance, *Random Papers*, Southwick, 1938.

Petworth Park and Pleasure Grounds: Historical Survey following the Great Storm of October 1987 (unpublished; funded by the National Heritage Memorial Fund).

ROWELL, Christopher, Ian WARRELL, and David BLAYNEY BROWN, *Turner at Petworth*, exh. cat., Petworth House, 2002.

ROWELL, Christopher, 'The North Gallery at Petworth: An Historical Re-appraisal', *Apollo*, cxxxviii, July 1993, pp. 29–36.

ROWELL, Christopher, 'The 2nd Earl of Egremont and Egremont House: A private London palace and its pictures', *Apollo*, cxlvii, April 1998, pp. 15–21.

ROWELL, Christopher, 'Grinling Gibbons's Carved Room at Petworth: "The most superb monument of his skill"', *Apollo*, cli, April 2000, pp. 19–26.

ROWELL, Christopher, 'Turner at Petworth: The 3rd Earl of Egremont's carved room restored', *Apollo*, clv, June 2002, pp. 40–7.

WAAGEN, Gustav, *Treasures of Art in Great Britain*, London, 1854, iii, pp. 31–43.

WOOD, Jeremy, 'The Architectural Patronage of Algernon Percy, 10th Earl of Northumberland' in *English Architecture Public and Private*, John Bold and Edward Chaney, eds., 1993, pp. 55–80.

WOOD, Jeremy, 'Van Dyck and the Earl of Northumberland: Taste and Collecting in Stuart England' in *Van Dyck 350*, S. Barnes and A. Wheelock, eds., Studies in the History of Art 46, National Gallery of Art, Washington, 1994, pp. 281–324.

WYNDHAM, Hugh, *A Family History 1688–1837: The Wyndhams of Somerset, Sussex and Wiltshire*, London, 1950.

WYNDHAM, Margaret, *Catalogue of the Collection of Greek and Roman Antiquities in the Possession of Lord Leconfield*, London, 1915.

YOUNGBLOOD, Patrick, 'That House of Art: Turner at Petworth', *Turner Studies*, ii, no. 2, 1983, pp. 16–33.